ADVENT!

World Events at the End of Time

LEWIS R. WALTON

REVIEW AND HERALD PUBLISHING ASSOCIATION
Washington, DC 20039-0555
Hagerstown, MD 21740

Copyright © 1986 by Review and Herald Publishing Association

Edited by Raymond H. Woolsey
Book design by Richard Steadham

Printed in U.S.A.

Library of Congress Cataloging in Publication Data

Walton, Lewis R.
  Advent! world events at the end of time.

  Includes bibliographical references.
  1. Second Advent. 2. Eschatology. 3. Seventh-day
Adventists—Doctrines. 4. Adventists—Doctrines.
I. Title.
BT886.W35 1986   236'.9   86-6505

ISBN 0-8280-0349-1

Dedicated

to
Lee R. Walton,
who taught me never to give up on
the Advent message—
and who now rests, waiting
for the Second Coming.

Contents

Prologue:
Thoughts at Sunset

It is sunset, and I am alone in the sky. Beyond the airplane windows, earth and air stretch out in wide panorama, a tumbled mixture of color and shadow, heralding the approach of night.

In the west a high curtain of clouds shatters the sun's last light, discarding everything except an orange so bright it seems to be made of neon. Far below, a rumpled blanket of coastal fog reflects the sunset. Somewhere beneath it lies the city of San Francisco.

I am going home after weekend meetings in northern California, and I find myself in the cramped, familar surroundings of my airplane. Out of habit I glance at the gauges on the instrument panel, at the turning engines, at the sky around me, and then I am again lost in thought. Once, not so very long ago, that low deck of fog would have protected San Francisco. In those days, just a generation ago, man's worst weapons were dependent upon human eyes for delivery.

Tonight San Francisco lies naked beneath its fog, only thirty minutes distant from the mysterious, armored silos punched deep into the soil of the Ukraine. Now its only safety lies in fear. The balance of terror: We are safe only if the other side is as frightened as we are.

"On earth nations will stand helpless, not knowing which way to turn . . . ; men will faint with terror" (Luke 21:25, 26, N.E.B.). The words come vividly to my mind. They were uttered two thousand years ago, but they describe the very world we live in.

"Nation will make war upon nation, kingdom upon kingdom; there will be great earthquakes, and famines . . . ; in the sky terrors and great portents" (verses 10, 11, N.E.B.). Someday, prophecy tells us, everything we have relied upon will vanish. Even the sky will seem filled with danger. And warnings of that oncoming event seem to be rising all around us, like pennants snapping in the wind.

Eleven thousand feet beneath me, the San Joaquin Valley slides into view—a fertile land filled with orchards and wheat and cotton. Unobstructed by coastal fog, it stretches out maplike, farms neatly marked by section lines and die-straight roads that sparkle in the early evening with distant headlights. From my vantage point high above the valley I see things in a new perspective. The people below me are like travelers bound together on the same ship—a beautiful but fragile ship, hurtling through both time and space. And the ship is headed for danger!

"I beheld the earth, and, lo, it was without form, and void. . . . I beheld, and, lo, there was no man, and all the birds of the heavens were fled. I beheld, and, lo, the fruitful place was a wilderness, and all the cities thereof were broken down" (Jer. 4:23-26). The words were penned six hundred years before the birth of Christ, but they describe something that will challenge the entire world.

This world: this beautiful valley beneath me, green from springtime's rains, warmed by the last glimmer of sunset. These people, gathering around supper tables, talking of their private dreams. But even as they do so, a dull fear nags at many of their minds. The future may be dangerous. Dreams may be out-of-date. People may, in fact, be better off tonight than they will ever be again.

And so, almost without realizing it, they are beginning to turn to the ultimate dream—that somewhere beyond this world may be a force that is able to help us. They watch *Star Wars* and *The Day After,* and turn a strange little creature called E.T. into a folk hero, as if they are now willing to accept help from any source that might offer a tonic for fear. Meanwhile, the pope emerges as a major world figure, able to draw thousands to any airport he visits.

Quite suddenly another thought sweeps over me, awesome with implications. Can it be that we are the generation of Adventists for whom time has finally run out? For nearly 150 years we have tried to give the message of Christ's return to a world where even professed Christians have mentally pushed His coming into some comfortably distant future. Up till now they could afford the luxury of doing that because however bad things might get, there was always some place to hide—some horizon to which a refugee could run. Tonight the last hiding place is gone. The security that diluted our sense of urgency is gone too. Is it possible that, at long last, the world is really ready to listen to the Advent message?

I look to the left. Just forward of the wing are the lights of Modesto, glimmering in the deepening twilight. Perhaps 150,000 people are down there in an area I can see with one casual glance. How many of them know the truth about the future? Have we really tried to tell them, or will we let them draw their hope from E.T., *Star Wars*, and the pope?

At night I usually fly at higher altitudes, to buy a little extra time and space should something go wrong. But now my altitude seems inappropriate. Two miles below me are people whose only hope of survival centers in the second coming of Christ. Is my distance from them a tragic symbol of where we have been for decades—a people blessed with truth, seeing the world with a panoramic view but so distant from it that our message has not gotten through?

Almost involuntarily my hand reaches for the throttles and slides them back. I descend, watching the landscape flatten around me until I can see the texture of people's lives: a car winding home in the gathering dusk, a tractor crawling over the final furrows of the day's last quarter section. Just ahead, wrapped in evening, a cluster of lights betrays an oncoming farm. In the bright glow of an outdoor security light I see washing on the line, a child's playhouse, an old pickup truck. It is there only for an instant, and then it is behind me—the humble bits and pieces of human lives.

Who will tell them?

And there is so much to tell! Everywhere one looks are signals that history is rapidly catching up with prophecy. Signals in the economic world, in the military world, in the world of religion.

"And he causeth all, both small and great, rich and poor, free and bond, to receive a mark" (Rev. 13:16). For decades we have known that someday world liberty would be threatened by centralized economic control. But do people realize how close we could be to that event? Do they know that everything necessary to bring about a classic Revelation 13 scenario has already happened?

My mind goes back to that summer day in southern Russia when I talked with the Moscow bureau chief of a well-known financial magazine. We were discussing a meeting that had taken place just a few days before, in which eleven debtor nations had conferred on what to do about a possible default on the huge debts they owe Western banks. With the soberest expression I had seen in a long time, he said to me, "If this means what it seems to mean, the whole Western financial structure is headed for a major shake-up."

Should his prediction come true, the United States could almost instantly find itself able to dictate economic policy to much of the world. I will explain why later on. For now, it is enough to say that if God should allow it, Revelation 13 could happen almost overnight. Its components are already in place, like a fully assembled machine, waiting only for some event to jar the switch—waiting for angels to release the winds of strife.

What about the increasingly dangerous world in which we live? At this moment Communism and capitalism are struggling for supremacy, and the conflict has moved as close as the mainland of Central America, less than 1,200 miles from Brownsville, Texas. The struggle has become global, and everyone agrees that it is exceedingly hazardous. But do they know that this too could be a fulfillment of prophecy? In the year 1903 an aging grandmother named

Ellen White described, with astonishing clarity, a situation that many feel could be applied to the Bolshevik revolution—an event that was still fourteen years in the future. She went on to predict that the spirit of revolution would spread until it tended to confront the "whole world." [1] Elsewhere she warned that "in the last scenes of this earth's history, war will rage." [2]

The economy. Social turmoil. Attempts at world revolution. The risk of war. We seem to be right on schedule, as though history were playing by a script. Is there anything else?

My thoughts drift to a recent event, in which the pope made still another visit to the Western Hemisphere. I remember the news stories and the thousands of upturned faces, worshipful in their hope that the Roman pontiff might bring an answer for their fears. I see that scene repeated in Poland and Costa Rica, Canada and the Solomon Islands. I see it in Anchorage, Alaska, and in Nicaragua.

"And his deadly wound was healed: and all the world wondered after the beast" (Rev. 13:3). The words drum in my brain like the steady rhythm of the airplane engines. There is no way I can avoid the conclusion: We must be nearing one of those dynamic times seen only rarely, in which the river of history jumps its banks, charting new territory, changing the whole course of world affairs. Something big lies ahead, just beyond the curtain of the future. People cannot see its details, but they can sense its presence, and millions are beginning to wonder what is coming.

We probably have never had a better chance to finish the work of God. Everything points to it. The quickening pace of history. The signals in the world around us. Even the hungry groping of millions of people who sense, without being quite able to say it, that our only hope lies in something like the coming of Christ. I believe that people are ready to listen to the Advent message. And to compound our good fortune, technology now enables us to

11

relay any newsworthy event to the entire globe simultaneously. In other words, the hardware is in place to finish the work of God with incredible speed.

I stare at the darkening sky around me, startled by the conclusion to which I have come. If all this means what I think it means, then this is the opportunity we have been dreaming of. Heaven is actually within reach. History is ready, waiting only for a response from the people of God.

And that, in turn, leads me to the most exciting thought of all. Everything necessary to prepare our lives for Christ's return can be done in an amazingly short period of time. We know that because of an event that happened in early Adventist history.

Few people are aware of it, but it seems that in the late 1850s the church came close to actually getting ready for the return of Christ. A deep revival swept across Adventism. Old wrongs were righted, differences between believers were healed. Even ministers made public confessions and pledges of reform. Apparently this triggered intense activity in heaven, for Ellen White described angels flying everywhere to prepare unbelieving hearts for truth. Soon revivals began to sweep secular America; noon prayer meetings sprang up in such unlikely places as the financial district of New York City, and newspaper editors got out special editions to describe the religious fervor that was spreading across the country. To this day, historians are at a loss to explain the phenomenon; it seems to have arisen spontaneously among laypeople, with little visible cause. But in the writings of Ellen White we get a fascinating glimpse beyond the veil, of heaven's mighty agencies rolling into action, going everywhere in response to reformation among the people of God.

Tragically, the reform did not last. Disappointed at not seeing results as quickly as they had hoped, many Adventists lost their commitment. And the work was not finished, and the Civil War rolled on like a juggernaut, and 500,000 men died at obscure towns such as Chancellorsville and Gettysburg, and history pressed on toward the nightmare of the twentieth century, and we have been left with a sad view of how expensive lost opportunities can be. But in the course of that brief revival Ellen White penned a statement that tells us just how quickly we *could* be ready to meet Jesus. Less than three years after the revival began, she said that it had had "time to do its work." In other words, within thirty-six months God's children could have been ready to meet Him!

Less than three years. That means that heaven is within our grasp. It is not some distant dream, receding before us like a mirage. We could actually have it—within the lifetime of nearly everyone now living!

I have been flying at low altitude for perhaps ten minutes. In that brief interval night has fallen thick around me, blotting out the horizon, shrinking my world to a few dots of light scattered here and there across the farmland. It is enough. I slide the throttles forward again, seeking height, watching the pinpricked darkness widen below me. I level off at 7,500 feet, but I do not reduce power. Relieved of its burden of climbing, the airplane surges forward, propellors biting at the air, clawing for speed.

Speed is what I want. Suddenly it is important to me to get home quickly. In a few moments of reflection I have realized that it is much later than we thought. The world military situation. The bizarre behavior of the economy. The resurgent right, urging a mixture of religion and politics. Even the doctrinal disputes within Adventism. It all fits. We are looking at an end-time scenario. History is trying to give birth to the coming of Jesus. Will we let it happen?

At my new altitude I can still see one thin, fading orange streak in the western sky. Beneath me the land is wrapped in darkness. It is sunset, when one begins to think of sleep.

But for me, the evening is different.

I am an Adventist.

It is the sunset of history.

And it is time to wake up.

13

Notes

[1] *Education*, p. 228.
[2] *Maranatha!*, p. 174.

Warnings
in the Wind

1 Pratt Valley is a narrow strip of land enclosed by
California's coastal mountains, and in the springtime
of 1909 there probably was not a more pleasant place in the
world. Beneath the steep bluff of Howell Mountain, the
valley sloped gently northward, radiant in the early-morn-
ing sun, fragrant with orchards and vineyards and the smell
of newly turned earth—as peaceful a location as one might
ever hope to find.

In a large home near the head of the valley lived an
aging grandmother, with dark-blue eyes and a wry sense of
humor. For all anyone could tell, she might have been
considerably younger than her 82 years. Each morning
after breakfast she could be seen out tromping around her
sixty-acre farm, inspecting the orchards and looking after
livestock. Despite her housekeeper's strident objections,
she was known, in moments of assertiveness, to go out into
the rain just to witness the arrival of a new calf. When she
was not inspecting her farm she was frequently out riding in
her buggy, and neighbors noticed that she drew a constant
stream of visitors—as though it just might be worth the
price of a train ticket to come and hear what this elderly
woman had to say.

In fact, she had a good deal to say about many things,
and not all of what she said was easy to listen to. Her name
was Ellen White. If one cared to believe her, there was a link
between disease and one's intake of animal fat. Tobacco,
she declared, was a "malignant poison." And she insisted
that the world everyone lived on—the real, tangible earth

beneath one's feet—was on borrowed time. Soon, she said, human affairs would collapse into a danger so great that even the most vivid imagination could not really picture it ahead of time.

In 1909 that was not a particularly believable point of view. America was at peace. The Stars and Stripes flew from Maine to Manila, and the future seemed headed straight for the stars. Though some nervous commentators worried about the crazy spiderweb of European military alliances, most people saw little reason for serious concern. Yet Ellen White clung stubbornly to her predictions of oncoming war. She declared bluntly that whole navies would go down and that millions of people were going to be lost. On occasion she even hinted at future weapons that would leave people with "no safety" anywhere on earth.[1]

That spring she was about to give yet another such warning. She was nearing completion of a new book, volume 9 of *Testimonies for the Church*, and its opening pages were filled with talk of future trouble. "We are living in the time of the end. The fast-fulfilling signs of the times declare that the coming of Christ is near at hand. . . . The calamities by land and sea, the unsettled state of society, the alarms of war, are portentious. They forecast approaching events of the greatest magnitude. . . .

"Great changes are soon to take place in our world, and the final movements will be rapid ones." [2]

Those changes might, in fact, be greater than most of her readers dreamed. She spoke of a "terrible conflict in the near future," of social injustice, of labor strife. Increasing crime would endanger everyone, "men, women, and little children," with acts so bizarre as to seem demonic. Frequent strikes would underscore the dangerous gulf between rich and poor. Along with decay in the social world she forecast trouble in the economy and described how leaders were "struggling in vain to place business operations on a more secure basis." [3]

That was not the worst of it. She also predicted that the world's cities would face a destructive force so powerful that man's defenses would be almost meaningless. "On one occasion, when in New York City," she wrote, "I was in the night season called upon to behold buildings rising story after story toward heaven." They were "warranted to be fireproof"; onlookers bragged that they were virtually indestructible—and if one judged things from then-known risks, they seemed to be. In the preceding twenty years great progress had been made in the use of concrete and structural steel; the new buildings were so strong that during World War II one skyscraper would withstand the direct impact of a multiengine airplane. Yet on that strange night in New York, Ellen White viewed the impossible: The indestructible buildings were in flames—and the fires could not be put out.[4]

"The scene that next passed before me was an alarm of fire. Men looked at the lofty and supposedly fireproof buildings and said: 'They are perfectly safe.' But these buildings were consumed as if made of pitch." A time was coming, she insisted, when "no material can be used in the erection of buildings that will preserve them from destruction." She described future emergencies in which fire fighters were helpless to stop the flames, because the "firemen were unable to operate the engines."[5]

For forty-one years that prediction waited in the opening pages of volume 9, so gloomy and apparently overstated that to believe it one had to accept the writings of Ellen White on a pretty large measure of faith. Buildings went up all over the world, built of brick and steel and the best that money could buy. Then on August 6, 1945, the city of Hiroshima burned to death after an atomic attack. Concrete and steel buildings disappeared beneath a fire that no human effort could stop. In the suburbs, blazing structures went untended because most of the city's fire fighting equipment was inoperable. The firemen were indeed "unable to operate the engines."[6]

Economic uncertainty. Increasing crime. The haunting specter of global-scale weapons. The warning lay there, clear and ominous, on the crisp new pages coming off the press at the publishing house; for anyone who cared to read it, the future was already written. Somewhere beyond the veil that hid tomorrow, beyond the sunlit springtime of 1909, beyond a safe America and a growing economy, beyond the dying fragments of Victorian morality, lay a future in which nothing would be secure anymore—not money, not morality, not one's neighborhood, not even the world itself, blue-white and shining beneath the peaceful sun, a sun whose awesome secrets of heat and energy would, within forty-three years, be harnessed by mankind in a thermonuclear bomb. The work of God would have to be finished with great speed, or the world would tumble off the edge into a deepening nightmare that Ellen White had repeatedly viewed and had tried to describe to a largely sleeping church.

"The tempest is coming," she had warned in 1890, "and we must get ready for its fury. . . . We shall see troubles on all sides. Thousands of ships will be hurled into the depths of the sea. Navies will go down, and human lives will be sacrificed by millions. Fires will break out unexpectedly, and no human effort will be able to quench them. . . . Confusion, collision, and death without a moment's warning will occur on the great lines of travel. The end is near, probation is closing. Oh, let us seek God while He may be found!" [7]

Fourteen years passed, and the warning came again, more urgent than ever. "Soon there will be death and destruction, increasing crime, and cruel, evil working against the rich who have exalted themselves against the poor. Those who are without God's protection will find no safety in any place or position. Human agents are being trained and are using their inventive power to put in operation the most powerful machinery to wound and to kill. . . . Let the means and the workers be scattered." [8]

Now it was 1909. Already an abortive revolt had flared briefly across Russia, jolting history with a hint of things to come. In Western Europe, nervous heads of state tromped into gilded and mirrored halls, fragrant with the scent of warm sealing wax, there to affix their hands and seals to military alliances that bound the world to war. In Germany, Count Alfred von Schlieffen's maps bore bold, westward-facing arrows that crossed Belgium and drove into the heart of France—the blueprint for oncoming World War I. And Ellen White, looking into an almost indescribable future, told of a scene that had passed before her in vision one memorable night, when she saw "an immense ball of fire fall upon some beautiful mansions, causing their instant destruction." The buildings apparently did not burn down—not in any sense one might use the term in 1909. They seem to have simply disappeared in an "instant." [9]

In a word, incredible. Beyond the gabled roofline of Elmshaven, Pratt Valley stretched off green and shimmering, alive with the silken light of a fog-washed morning. Horses moved at a slow trot, carrying farm families toward nearby St. Helena, and though the round trip couldn't have been much more than ten miles, most folks planned to spend the better part of the day on a trip to town.

No safety in any place or position? Beyond St. Helena lay San Francisco Bay, and beyond that, the Pacific Ocean—64 million square miles of moated emptiness, guarding America's western frontier. To the east, the Atlantic provided a buffer from Europe's conflicts, while northward the landscape faded out into the forbidding shield of the polar cap. Trouble could never come from that direction—could it? Yet Ellen White had described a world in which there was no place left to hide.

Admittedly, this was not particularly easy to believe, and there were any number of people who were ready to write off such doomsaying as the ramblings of a misguided woman. Some of her harshest critics were, in fact, either in the church or on its fringes. Back in 1889 an apostate Adventist minister named D. M. Canright had trumpeted the charge that she was a fraud, suffering from nervous disorders while plagiarizing much of what she wrote. In the early twentieth century Dr. John Harvey Kellogg had been saying things that sounded very much the same, as had Albion Ballenger, a disgruntled ex-minister who passionately disagreed with her on the subject of the heavenly sanctuary. All this had produced no small turmoil in Adventism, where critics of Mrs. White had also recently begun challenging some of the most basic concepts of the Advent message. The conflict had grown so intense that even some seasoned workers had been swept off into doctrinal confusion, and such people did not go without followers. It was, after all, considerably easier to hear them criticize Ellen White than to listen to her uncomfortable challenges, and thus Adventists were being forced steadily toward an important decision. Would they opt for the soothing reassurances of articulate speakers, whose criticism coincided so handily with human inclination, or would they continue to believe the Spirit of Prophecy—with its strange portrayals of oncoming war, a world-threatening revolution, economic crisis, and balls of fire that could wreak instant destruction?

So the church waited, numbed by challenge and by controversy, shaken by its recent collision with a massive apostasy called the "alpha," in which some of its brightest lights had gone out. People could not see it yet, but already the shades of night were gathering. Within five years World War I would blaze across Europe, forever changing the direction of history. There was still a little time, but now time was the most precious commodity in the world. Soon it would be gone; the chance to finish God's work in peace and prosperity would be gone with it, and a golden moment would vanish, leaving a fragmented world in which large areas would be inaccessible, for a time, to the gospel.

All that was happening in the springtime of 1909. Meanwhile, half a world away, two men were moving out of the shadows and into the mainstream of history.

One was a brilliant young German Jew by the name of Albert Einstein.

The other was a bald, icy-eyed, revolutionary who went by the name of Nikolai Lenin.

Notes

[1] *Signs of the Times,* April 21, 1890; *Testimonies,* vol. 8, p. 50.
[2] *Testimonies,* vol. 9, p. 11.
[3] *Ibid.,* p. 13.
[4] *Ibid.,* pp. 12, 13.
[5] *Ibid.,* p. 13.
[6] *Ibid.*
[7] *Signs of the Times,* April 21, 1890.
[8] *Testimonies,* vol. 8, p. 50.
[9] *Ibid.,* vol. 9, p. 28.

The Storm Approaches

2 Albert Einstein was a striking young man, darkly handsome, with a cropped black mustache and soft eyes that seemed focused somewhere beyond infinity; in the springtime of 1909 he was already a rising star. Though only 30 that March, he was sought by a growing number of European scientists who couldn't have failed to notice that this brilliant young man was also amazingly absent-minded. (Once, in later life, he spent an embarrassing day holding up his pants while trying to write formulas on the blackboard for a classroom full of students; he had forgotten to put on his belt.) But there was a reason for his faraway gaze and his disregard for daily trivia. Albert Einstein's eyes were indeed focused on infinity, and his insights were about to plunge the world over the brink on a long and ultimately terrifying downhill run toward danger.

For some time he had been thinking about the universe, pondering what relationships might govern this vast expanse of space and matter, and he had reached a conclusion that was enough to bend anyone's mind. There was energy locked in matter, he said—so much energy that to express it mathematically one would have to use an exponent of the speed of light.

Light moved at an almost incomprehensible speed. It could travel from moon to earth in just over one second. In less than nine minutes it could go the distance between earth and sun—93 million miles away. But Einstein was saying that the energy stored in matter was greater still, so vast that it involved the speed of light squared. In other words, the ratio of energy to mass was more than 34 billion to one. If mankind could ever find a way to unlock it, they would produce the biggest explosion history had ever seen.

His theory gradually began to draw the attention of other physicists and engineers, men who could take an abstraction and translate it into hardware . In America, Germany, even Russia, scientists played with this fascinating monster, poking at the atom with mathematical formulas and with cyclotrons, to see if the energy stored there just might be released. World War II came. German engineers gathered material for a nuclear experiment. Meanwhile, American scientists, in the supersecret Manhattan Project, began working on a device of their own. And one July day in 1945 the thing was ready to be tested.

On the morning of July 16, 1945, just before dawn, the world's first nuclear explosion was triggered atop a hundred-foot steel tower in the New Mexico desert . The event "beggared description. The whole country was lighted by a searing light with an intensity many times that of the midday sun. It was golden, purple, violet, gray, and blue. It lighted every peak, crevasse, and ridge with a clarity and beauty that cannot be described." From a distance of more than five miles, one observer described a "strong sensation of heat on the exposed skin of the face and arms," while another gazed in wonderment at the "reddish glowing smoke ball rising with a thick stem of dark brown"—mankind's first look at the familiar mushroom cloud.[1] It was some time before awestruck observers noticed that the hundred-foot steel tower was gone. It had vaporized in the explosion; beneath it, desert sand had turned to glass.

Three weeks later a similar device was triggered over the city of Hiroshima. A flash of light preceded a concussion so enormous that the stone pillars outside the Shima medical clinic were driven into the ground. Searing heat reached down to touch the city with flame, while in the suburbs a mysterious wall of hardened air hammered outward, flattening homes and sending glass rocketing like shrapnel. As the noise died out, a funnel in the sky drew part of the shattered city upward, tons of pulverized debris riding an enormous column of heat. For a time the cloudy pillar stood over the desolated landscape like a visitor from some fiery realm, lingering as if to savor the moment of its release.

J. R. Oppenheimer, a physicist who had worked on the atomic project, said, "I am become death, the destroyer of worlds."

In the springtime of 1909 E. G. White had described an "immense ball of fire" that caused "instant destruction," and she had begged God's people to work before it was too late. "If every soldier of Christ had done his duty, . . . " she had said sadly, "the world might ere this have heard the message of warning. But the work is years behind. While men have slept, Satan has stolen a march upon us." [2] Now it was 1945. Thirty-six years had passed, and the price of their passing was going up. Hiroshima lay dead beneath the August sun, her center gone, large areas as level as a plowed field. On the hills and ridges near the city, trees turned yellow, as if in an instant autumn. And in the suburbs, fires continued to burn. The firemen were "unable to operate the engines."

Seven hundred years before Christ the prophet Isaiah had penned a passage that now took on sobering implications. "Fear, and the pit, and the snare, are upon thee, O inhabitant of the earth. And it shall come to pass, that he who fleeth from the noise of the fear shall fall into the pit; and he that cometh up out of the midst of the pit shall be taken in the snare: for the windows from on high are opened, and the foundations of the earth do shake" (Isa. 24:17, 18). He described how the "earth is utterly broken down" (verse 19), and he included a passage filled with gloomy relevance for anyone living after 1945: "Therefore the inhabitants of the earth are burned, and few men left" (verse 6).

The "noise of fear." Danger coming from "on high," seeming to shake Earth's very foundations. People fleeing into the "pit." More hazards awaiting as they climbed out. What *was* Isaiah saying? Was this just Old Testament allegory, confined to the time of Israel? Or was it a warning that sin, left to itself, could one day be frighteningly self-destructive? A clue can be found in the writings of Ellen White.

In the opening pages of volume 9 of the *Testimonies*, Ellen White referred to this chapter in Isaiah and associated it with reference to war—war that still lay in the future! "The world is stirred with the spirit of war," she said, just before quoting Isaiah 24. "The prophecy of the eleventh chapter of Daniel has nearly reached its complete fulfillment. Soon the scenes of trouble spoken of in the prophecies will take place." A few paragraphs later she said it all again. "The spirit of war is stirring the nations from one end of the earth to the other." Soon, she said, the world would see "a time of trouble such as has not been since there was a nation," during which God's people would have to depend for protection upon "angels that excel in strength." [3]

Soon, but not yet. In the springtime of 1909 all this still lay in the future, as Pratt Valley farmers rattled toward St. Helena in flatbed wagons, horse-drawn and laden with the cabbages and turnips of winter gardens. So much was coming; so much, so soon. The forces of history were converging, pushing mankind into a narrowing canyon from which, at last, there would be no escape except the coming of Jesus. Already young Einstein was dazzling Europe with his unparalleled insight into matter and energy, hastening humanity toward its rendezvous with a dreadful ball of fire. And meanwhile the world was racing toward another challenge—a revolution, urged on by a driving, relentless Russian named Nikolai Lenin.

By any standard of logic, Lenin should never have been a revolutionary. Born as Vladimir Ulyanov, he was the son of a respected government official, whose family enjoyed privileges most Russians never had. Logically, he should have followed his father into government service, disappearing into the maze of czarist bureaucracy, unrecognized by history. But logic did not count for much anymore. Great changes were coming upon the world, and nothing would ever be the same again. Somewhere in the turbulence of a changing era, young Lenin became a passionate, fire-breathing revolutionary whose one goal in life was to destroy the status quo.

Years earlier, a Russian anarchist named Sergey Nechayev had penned some chilling advice on how to change the world. His ideas are worth looking at for a moment because they reveal, with terrible clarity, part of the reason why we live in such a dangerous world. According to Nechayev, the only hope for humanity was the violent destruction of existing world order; any available weapon was acceptable if it hastened the revolution. That included terror, assassination, even the sacrifice of innocent people.

"The revolutionary knows that in the very depths of his being . . . he has broken all the bonds which tie him to the social order and the civilized world. . . . He despises and hates the existing social morality. . . . Night and day he must have but one thought, one aim—merciless destruction." [4]

The revolutionary, Nechayev declared, italicizing his words for emphasis, "should not hesitate to destroy any position, any place, or any man in this world." He must "penetrate everywhere," into business, government, even churches, pretending to be a part of the system while secretly planning its destruction. He spoke openly of assassination, glowing over the way that "violent and sudden deaths will produce the utmost panic in government." [5]

Nechayev went to his death, but his ideas were picked up by Lenin, who embraced them with evangelical fervor. In the springtime of 1909 he was hard at work planning a revolution that would sweep Russia and challenge the world.

And six years earlier, Ellen White wrote in terms as if

she were telling her church exactly what he was doing!

In 1903, her book *Education* had come off the press. Primarily a guide for the training of Christian young people, it nonetheless contained one of the most impressive predictions of the twentieth century. Hidden beneath the troubled surface of human affairs, she said, trends were developing that would challenge global order. The poorer people of the world would unite, struggling to overthrow the power of the rich. Anarchy would be seen. And in the process, the world would be challenged by the same doctrines that produced the French Revolution—atheism and materialism.

"Anarchy is seeking to sweep away all law, not only divine, but human. The centralizing of wealth and power; the vast combinations for the enriching of the few at the expense of the many; the combinations of the poorer classes for the defense of their interests and claims; . . . the worldwide dissemination of the same teachings that led to the French Revolution—all are tending to involve the whole world in a struggle similar to that which convulsed France." [6]

Similar to that which convulsed France. That revolution was characterized by the overthrow of royalty, assassination of the royal family, forfeiture of wealth, seizure of church property, and official promulgation of atheism as the religion of the state.

The French Revolution followed the reign of a weak and ineffective monarch who was married to a foreign-born queen. In his waning days the French king struggled to regain order—sometimes by force, sometimes by grudging concessions. His efforts, however, seemed only to make matters worse. Anarchy swept the French country-side, and armed peasants burst into landlords' homes, where they burned the records of their feudal debts. Land was forcibly taken and redistributed. Church properties were seized. In Paris, churches were closed, and public religious services severely constrained.

The king tried to flee, was caught, tried, and executed.

Then came the "Terror." The queen was guillotined. Many other political figures met the same fate. The philosophy behind all this turmoil turned out to be atheism coupled with materialism—a rejection of religion, and a belief only in that which could be humanly seen, touched, and measured.

Whether Ellen White specifically had Russia in mind and was comparing it to France, we do not know, but the analogy certainly is close. Change "king" to "czar" and "Paris" to "Petrograd," and everything fits—even to Russia's "Red Terror," so reminiscent of the postrevolu--tionary turmoil seen in France. Even to the atheism and materialism, also urged by Karl Marx in his *Communist Manifesto!*

Thus in 1903, Ellen White had foreseen something like the Russian Revolution and had described it so clearly that no one need have been taken by surprise. There would be attempts at a great worldwide change, fed by the seething frustrations of the world's poor and led by people who admitted their willingness to destroy any position, place, or man in this world. If, during that period of global struggle, mankind developed the weapons Ellen White had predicted—world-threatening weapons, leaving "no safety in any place or position"—there would indeed be no safe place left on earth. Someday, sooner or later, people would confront the stark truth that without the coming of Jesus, the human race was doomed.

She was not the only writer to suggest that something like this was coming. Nearly nineteen centuries earlier the apostle James had penned a blunt warning of turmoil at the end of time.

"Now listen, you rich people, weep and wail because of the misery that is coming upon you. Your wealth has rotted. . . . your gold and silver are corroded. Their corrosion will . . . eat your flesh like fire." He said that social injustice would be "crying out against you" and added a gloomy description of a "day of slaughter" (James 5:1-5, N.I.V.). The world described by James is a paradox of wealth and poverty. Some enjoy a very high standard of living while others are hungry. Something goes terribly wrong. The whole system seems to tumble inverted, so that the once-sought status of wealth instead attracts danger, and one's net worth seems to "rot"—a metaphor that at least suggests hyperinflation and economic collapse. As the structure crumbles, violent forces are released that are described by James as a "day of slaughter." And he predicted that all this would happen late in human history, in the "last days."

Christ Himself had made a similar statement, in which He foretold a time of "great distress. . . . On the earth, nations will be in anguish and perplexity. . . . Men will faint from terror, apprehensive of what is coming on the world"(Luke 21:23-26, N.I.V.). Over and over the warnings had come, some dating deep into Jewish antiquity; and now, at the dawn of the twentieth century, Ellen White was saying that the long-awaited time of turmoil was about to begin. "Soon there will be death and destruction, increasing crime, and cruel, evil working against the rich who have exalted themselves against the poor." Without supernatural protection, one would find "no safety" anywhere on earth.[7]

For a time her predictions waited in the pages of volumes 8 and 9 of the *Testimonies,* all too often ignored by the very people for whom time was running out. But little by little the sky of history began to darken. In 1904—the very year in which volume 8 was published—Japan and Russia went to war. Desperate to salvage defeats in Asia, the czar ordered his Baltic fleet on a suicidal journey around the tip of Africa. Japan's Admiral Togo defeated them, destroying what was left of Russia's naval war machine. The war was lost, and ripples of revolt swept across Russia. In his excitement, Lenin even dared a brief return to Russia after European exile. A dress rehearsal had taken place for events that would soon shake the world.

The warning signals were there—in prophecy, in world events—but all too few cared to look at them. In America, crowds at Coney Island's Castle Summer House danced until dawn. In England, policymakers cast occasional nervous glances at Germany's mighty new navy, but calmed themselves with the thought that if the German fleet were impressive, the map of the world was even more so: Fully a quarter of the globe bore the ensign of Britain's empire. And then, when people spoke wistfully of peace, a new storm began approaching—black and hard against the sky of August, 1914, built of towering thunderheads that gave off the rumble of approaching gunfire. This time the storm could not be slept through. It would be called World War I, and before it was over, 10 million soldiers would lie dead at places such as the Marne and Verdun, and Russia would blaze with revolution.

"The unsettled state of society, the alarms of war, are portentous," Ellen White had written, and she had warned that the future held the seeds of "anarchy." [8] Now it was here; the juggernaut was over the summit, accelerating ponderously on a downhill run that offered no visible stopping place. From this point on, nothing mankind could do—not the League of Nations, not the United Nations, not the sacrifice of a hundred million lives—would stop the engine of human self-destruction. It would roll wildly on, gathering energy from each new crisis, until it crashed headlong into the nuclear age.

It is August, 1945. Above the city of Hiroshima a lone B-29 bomber drops a simple bomb and then races away as if to run from something. Seconds later the morning sky fills with hot white light—a light that scorches the last thread of human innocence. The world tumbles crazily into strange new circumstances.

In divided Europe, more than 400,000 square miles pass behind a barrier that comes to be called the iron curtain. World War II's allies drift apart, jockeying for power, worried for the future. Secure behind his nuclear monopoly, President Truman massively disarms, retaining only fifteen Army divisions. Premier Stalin, his mind filled with memories of the cloud over Hiroshima, retains Soviet readiness with 175 divisions. And deep within Russian security, engineers work on their first nuclear weapon.

It is detonated on the last Monday in August, 1949.

That year will be a memorable one for the forces that dream of world revolution. Scarcely two months after the Soviet nuclear test, Marxist forces sweep China. Victorious Maoists sing, "The East is Red," and sweep away wealthy landowners in a purge that costs 800,000 lives, a grim reminder of James's prophecy about a "day of slaughter." In this step, world Communism gains control of a half billion people. And within a year the west is challenged by an armed invasion of South Korea.

As South Korea is invaded, the world, in the name of the United Nations, goes to war. For three years combat rages on the Korean peninsula. Nearly 6 million Americans serve; more than 50,000 do not return. The war is essentially a stalemate.

And then on October 4, 1957, Americans are startled to learn that the first man-made satellite has been launched by the Soviet Union. Suddenly Russian claims of technical skill can no longer be conveniently dismissed. This is not unfounded bragging; this is real. One hundred and eighty-four pounds of Soviet hardware are in earth orbit. If Russian rockets can do that, they can go anywhere on earth.

The 1960s speed by in a blur, melting into the 1970s. Cuba. Berlin. China's first nuclear test. (Its fourth nuclear test is delivered by a missile.) Vietnam. Angola. Afghanistan.

And Ethiopia, and the horn of Africa, and Nicaragua, and El Salvador—and the conflict is established on the American continent, less than 1,200 miles from Texas. It has spread until it does indeed tend to "involve the whole world."

Meanwhile, just as predicted, weapons have progressed almost beyond imagination. A single rocket can now carry ten bombs across the world with such accuracy that each falls within three hundred yards of its intended target. In space, spy satellites cross and recross the earth, scanning the surface, capable of recognizing objects as small as two feet—from an altitude of two hundred miles ! Even poor countries burden their fragile economies with the cost of jet-age arms. One's mind goes back to the pointed prophecy of Joel: "Proclaim this among the nations: Prepare for war! Rouse the warriors! . . . Beat your plowshares into swords and your pruning hooks into spears. Let the weakling say, 'I am strong' " (Joel 3:9, 10, N.I.V.).

Wealth and poverty. Attempts at world revolution. Unification of revolutionaries around atheism and materialism. A world arms race that is now entering space. The predictions could not have been more accurate if they had been written yesterday.

Which means that there is absolutely no reason to worry. God has not forgotten us, and history is not happening by accident. It is following prophecy like a script. We are exactly where we were predicted to be.

But that does not mean it is a time for getting comfortable. History has also closed the circle on us. We are out of time. Today, there is no rational alternative to the coming of Christ. God's people, so long in the wilderness, now have no real choice but to make the Advent a reality.

It is time, at last, to get serious about the Advent message.

Notes

[1] Anthony Cave Brown and Charles B. McDonald, *The Secret History of the Atomic Bomb* (New York: Dial Press, 1977), p. 516.

[2] *Testimonies*, vol. 9, p. 29.

[3] *Ibid.*, pp. 14, 17.

[4] Robert Payne, *The Life and Death of Lenin* (New York: Simon and Schuster, 1964), pp. 24, 25.

[5] *Ibid.*

[6] *Education*, p. 228.

[7] *Testimonies*, vol. 8, p. 50.

[8] *Ibid.*, vol. 9, p. 11; *Education*, p. 228.

"That No Man Might Buy or Sell"

3 As the coming of Jesus nears, world events will assume a distinctive pattern foretold by prophecy. Like the profile of a graph, history will reveal recognizable peaks and valleys. Valleys of danger: economic constraint, military threat, religious confusion, the desperation of a Sunday law. Peaks of opportunity: revival and reformation, the latter rain, the gospel to the world.

In recent years something fascinating has been happening. Little by little, that distinctive profile has begun to appear—sometimes openly, sometimes cleverly disguised. The military danger, so graphically described by apostles and prophets, has clearly arrived; it has muscled its way into our lives, unwanted but irresistible, giving mankind the globe-threatening power described in Revelation 11. With it, just as Ellen White predicted, has come a major effort at revolution, "tending to involve the whole world." Today we live each hour under the shadow of those combined threats.

But while the military danger was forcing its way into history, another problem has stolen in almost unnoticed, as quietly and imperceptibly as predawn fog. It is an economic threat, and its stealthy arrival is deceptive, for within it are the seeds of world turmoil worse than anything short of global war. It is the crisis spoken of in Revelation 13.

"And he causeth all, both small and great, rich and poor, free and bond, to receive a mark. . . . And that no man might buy or sell, save he that had the mark, or the name of the beast, or the number of his name" (Rev. 13:16, 17).

For generations Adventists have believed that something like this is coming—that late in human history mankind will try a catastrophic experiment in global control, in which some centralized power will attempt to regulate the lives of everyone on earth. Even the wealthy will be required to obey—a broad indication that this development involves a crisis so severe that wealth seems irrelevant. And the leverage for enforcement will be the world economy.

We have waited for that event decade after decade, in a state of high expectation, welcoming each world crisis as a sure sign of the end. And as we did so, a subtle emotional mechanism has operated within Adventism: We have found that it is impossible to preserve a crisis mentality indefinitely. For a time the stimulation of challenge may goad us to high acts, but when the challenge is delayed and the stimulation dies, we find ourselves to be very ordinary human beings. We speak wistfully of the end of time, but more and more we drift into a dependence on the very world we profess to be leaving.

In other words, what we need is not a relationship with crisis, but a relationship with Christ.

Not surprisingly, as the decades have passed and He has not returned, some in Adventism have begun to question whether our understanding of Revelation 13 is really correct. And therein lies a double irony: While we waited—and wondered—the real thing has stolen into our lives so cleverly that most people never saw it come. To put it bluntly, everything necessary to bring about a classic Revelation 13 scenario is already here—waiting, like a fully assembled machine, for some event to turn it on.

And it has all happened in the past ten years.

I am going to go into some detail about how it happened, not necessarily because we are on the verge of a Revelation 13 crisis, but to show you how a whole series of events, seemingly disconnected from each other, can combine to create a situation in which prophecy could be fulfilled with great speed.

Go back a few years. It is the summer of 1973. U.S.

troops have left Vietnam. With the exception of Watergate, American life is returning to normal. And at the gasoline pump one can purchase auto fuel for only 34.9 cents a gallon. People do not realize it at the time, but the cost of fuel is one of the most important factors in their lives. If the energy price structure cracks, the way will be open for a whole series of economic troubles. Interest rates will soar; so will inflation. Americans will learn strange terms such as *stagflation*. Recession will rob large groups of their hard-won economic benefits. Things will never be quite the same again.

But in the summer of 1973, doomsayers are not particularly believable, for one can fill a gasoline tank for $5, and the posted speed limit on many highways is 70 miles per hour. It is summertime, and the living is easy.

Then autumn came. On the eve of Yom Kippur, 1973, crack Egyptian units climbed aboard personnel carriers and headed east toward the Israeli defense lines beyond the Suez Canal. The Middle East was at war, and the effects of that war reached into the very heart of American life. Angered at Western support of Israel, Arab nations did something heretofore seen mostly in State Department nightmares—they turned off the oil supply to the West. In America, cars lined up for blocks to buy scarce and increasingly expensive fuel. Unrecognized as such, an event had arrived capable of setting the stage for a fulfillment of Revelation 13.

As the price of oil soared far beyond its cost of production, a relatively few nations found themselves awash in money—so much money that it is difficult to comprehend. In a single week, the nations in the Organization of Petroleum Exporting Countries (OPEC) took in enough funds to buy every newspaper and broadcast station in America. In just thirty weeks, these nations earned a sum equal to the value of every stock listed on the London Stock Exchange. And almost immediately they began to face a problem: Just what does one do with such a huge volume of cash?

The answer they decided upon was logical enough: Deposit their surplus in the world's largest banks, multinational giants able to arrange huge loans, thus generating interest income on their funds. The plan had a side benefit. Industry, reeling from energy price increases, would have plenty of money to borrow while adapting to the new cost of fuel.

All in all, not a bad plan. It just might have worked, except . . .

Except that the economy, wracked by the skyrocketing cost of energy, was plunging into the deepest recession since the 1930s. As a result, there simply weren't enough borrowers to use all the money OPEC was depositing. Instead, thousands of workers were laid off, deepening the recession with decreased buying power. Thus the world passed into a time of weird economic trouble: stubborn recession, the humbling of once-mighty trade unions, a federal deficit approaching $200 billion a year, and people wondering about the security of their pensions and savings.

The burden of wealth had passed from the oil producers to the banks, and it quickly proved to carry with it a mysterious curse. In Saudi Arabia, it had drawn problems the way a magnet draws tacks. Threats to the Muslim social system. Threats from itinerate workers, who toiled in the 120°F. heat and wondered why the fabulous wealth of the Ghawar oil field should be controlled by a royal family. Threats from Ethiopia and south Yemen, where dark and mysterious forces of revolution moved in the shadows, accompanied by bearded advisers who spoke with Cuban accents. Threats from the West, where military planners briefly laid out their maps and wondered what it would be like to turn the oil fields over to the Marines. And threats from the Soviet Union, whose interest in the area was finally revealed in an invasion that did get past the paper stage—a thrust into nearby Afghanistan.

All that for the sake of an oil price rise. Oil had turned to gold, and the gold was beginning to give off corrosive fumes, as if it were brewing up something filled with menace. Now wealth's troublesome responsibility passed to the multinational bankers, who were about to learn for themselves just how disagreeable so much money could be.

The bankers' problem was serious. They had large sums of Arab money, upon which they had to pay interest, but there were too few borrowers generating income for the banks. A solution suggested itself: If private business could not use all the available loan funds, what about governments—whole countries? Sovereign nations? What about Poland, and Brazil, and Argentina, and Mexico? Nothing could be safer than a loan to a sovereign country—could it?

Before anyone really knew what was happening, three Western Hemisphere nations alone owed more money than was owned by the stockholders of America's nine largest banks. And then the bottom fell out. World recession struck again. Interest rates soared. Whole nations, mortgaged up to their capitols, couldn't even meet their interest payments.

This was no longer some distant problem that one could read about in detached comfort, while drinking dollar-a-cup coffee on the fortieth floor. This could touch America. Several hundred billion dollars had disappeared, like a flight of birds, into the steamy jungles and dusty towns of countries that were as much as bankrupt. It could take more than a miracle to bring those dollars home again. And if they didn't return, some of the largest banks in the world might face losses they couldn't cover.

All of which pushed the banking community to a grim game of "what if." What if a major debtor nation did collapse? Worse yet, what if the world's poorer nations united, repudiating their debts all at once? Thus far, bankers had played a delicate game, pretending that the loans were still collectible. On occasion, when interest payments were due, they would even make further loans, thus enabling their insolvent borrowers to "pay" the interest with more borrowed money. But if some country finally blew the whistle, repudiating its indebtedness altogether, the game would be over. In the computerized, disk-driven journals of the lending banks, a repudiated debt shifts from "nonperforming" to "uncollectible." It has become an actual loss, and the loss has to be recognized.

Except that it is not a $47,000 loan with a first mortgage on someone's house. It is a ten-digit figure, and there may not be money enough in the bank to cover it. If the idea spreads to other debtor countries, if dominoes tumble, there may not be funds enough in the whole banking system to cover the loss.

That is international economic doomsday. It is panic in the world stock exchanges, and bank lines two blocks long. It is printing presses running three shifts at the Bureau of Printing and Engraving, and the Dow Jones falling like a grand piano, and world trade catastrophically interrupted. It is Revelation 13, jarred into action, leading the United States straight into global economic dominance. Let me explain.

Recently I was en route to Moscow on a business trip. In Amsterdam I picked up a newspaper that instantly cured my jet lag. On the front page was a report of a recent meeting by the major debtor nations in the Western Hemisphere, in which they planned how best to meet the international debt crisis. As I read the article, one predominant fact emerged: They intended to stand together, bargaining as a unit.

In southern Russia I attended a meeting with a man who is the Moscow bureau chief for a major American financial magazine, and I asked his reaction to the news. "This ," he said, "is the event we have been dreading. If they do unify, it could be OPEC in reverse—a debtor's cartel, where the debtors dictate policy to the lenders. If the worst happens, if they all go at once, we are in for the deepest shakeup since the 1930s."

When we consider this in the light of Revelation 13, we can see how that prophecy *could* be fulfilled. Oddly enough, an international banking crisis could catapult the United States to unprecedented economic dominance—and for a very simple reason: only the United States can print dollars.

If the worst should occur, and major lenders should face losses they could not cover, the world economy would probably react much like a living organism after a massive hemorrhage. The dollar serves as a primary vehicle for world trade, and hundreds of millions of dollars would have vanished—into failed crops and private jets and half-built nuclear reactors in the Third World. Only an immediate transfusion of dollars could revive the organism of global commerce, and only one entity in the world—the United States Federal Reserve System board of directors—could authorize creation of the money.

So financial strategists have discussed a plan. In a worst-case scenario, America would create enough new money to meet the losses; it would then lend it to the world's failed banks so that they could resume business. To put it another way, America would become lender of last resort to the world. It would hold the mortgage on global commerce. It could dictate policy to a degree rarely seen in history.

"And he causeth all, both small and great, rich and poor, . . . to receive a mark . . . And that no man might buy or sell, save he that had the mark . . . or the number" (Rev. 13:16, 17). John's prophecy no longer has to be relegated to the distant future. The machinery is in place. To an astonishing degree, we have lost control of our global economy. Some otherwise insignificant event in the Third World could precipitate the scene foretold by John.

Now for a caution, and I am going to italicize it for emphasis. *None of this means that history will follow the script you have just read.* Indeed, final events will probably be much more complex than anything we now imagine. Those who attempt to say exactly how prophecy will be fulfilled are engaging in risky speculation, for at least two reasons. First, we have no idea of the extent to which heaven will intervene to prevent crises that to us seem rather certain. God often alters events to allow people the gift of time.

The second factor is the response (or lack thereof) by God's people. At least twice before in the history of Adventism a clearly recognizable end-time pattern has begun to develop. In the 1850s, and again near the turn of the century, events occurred that make it pretty clear that Jesus was trying to return. In the 1890s Ellen White declared that the latter rain had begun; Sunday legislation was widely proposed in America, and the Adventist health message drew widespread attention—even from such famed persons as Henry Ford and Harvey Firestone. But a tragic apostasy called the "alpha" swept through the church, destroying a clear opportunity to finish the work in a time of real opportunity. [1] The moment was lost, and the nightmare of the twentieth century dawned, and we are still in this world.

So the current debt crisis may mean everything—and it may mean nothing. What you have just read is not an attempt to predict the future. It is just one illustration (out of many possible examples) showing how a thousand different nightly news stories, apparently unconnected with each other, can combine to create a situation ripe for classic Adventist eschatology. Unless you have your heart and mind deep in the Bible and the Spirit of Prophecy, you might never recognize these events until they are all around you. If you are really interested in studying last-day events in the Spirit of Prophecy, the book *Maranatha!* is one of the finest volumes you can buy. It ought to be read and reread until it is worn out. And then a new copy ought to be bought and read some more.

The future will be filled with surprises, but we can say one thing with certainty: Warning signals are clear. If we cannot see them, our banker friends can.

Meanwhile, two other elements of John's prophecy also deserve thoughtful attention. One of them is the prediction that government will regulate the behavior of everyone on earth, controlling even such day-to-day essentials as buying and selling. The other is the prophecy that government will enforce religious legislation. Like the international debt crisis, these too have crept by inches into our lives. Forces able to bring them about are now here, in the form of electronic banking and a highly political religious right.

"THAT NO MAN MIGHT BUY OR SELL"

In 1946 the U.S. Army began using one of the world's first electronic computers. Nicknamed ENIAC, it was a monstrous device: its 18,000 vacuum tubes required 140,000 watts of electrical power and filled several rooms. Yet it could work complex calculations in a fraction of a second. Ten years later the transistor revolutionized electronics. Ten more years passed, and engineers developed something called microcircuitry, shrinking circuits that once filled entire rooms to a chip the size of a fingernail. Today computers with the power of ENIAC can be put in one's pocket.

With the remarkable growth of data processing has come a whole new way of shopping, in which laser-equipped cash registers recognize your purchase, compute the price, and print a receipt showing exactly what you bought. (Have you ever wondered how much of that data a computer might choose to remember?) If you use a credit card, you are so well known to the system that in many stores, data terminals can almost instantly verify your credit. From where we are right now it would be a short step to a totally cashless society, in which you would never need to touch money physically, and your net worth would become a series of digital entries in a bank's computer disks. If that should happen, your only source of spending power could become an electronically encoded card, without which you might find yourself unable to buy even the basic necessities of life.

In blunt fact, a system suggestive of that described in Revelation is already here. We have welcomed it into our lives, lured by convenience, not stopping to realize that the same system that makes buying easy could also be used to make buying impossible. The equipment is already in place!

Meanwhile, events in the world of religion have moved rapidly, carrying us in just twenty years further than many people thought we would ever go. As one looks back, the process seems to begin with a personable, handsome young politician named John F. Kennedy.

In 1960, when John Kennedy won his party's nomination for President, he faced an obstacle that no one had ever overcome: He was a Catholic, and predominantly Protestant America had never allowed a Catholic anywhere near the Presidency. But Kennedy felt that the nation might be ready for a change in religious thinking. A new era of tolerance was dawning, and with it came the first glimmer of possibility that anti-Catholic sentiment could be overcome. He plunged into the campaign with gusto, confronting the religion issue head-on. The landmark event in that struggle came in Houston, Texas, when Kennedy spoke to a Protestant ministerial association, challenging them so passionately for tolerance that the religion issue died almost overnight. Suddenly no one dared to voice anti-Catholic sentiment. Kennedy won the election, and millions of Americans who had never seen the inside of a Catholic church found themselves traveling, via television, to mass each Sunday with this attractive young President, whose family drew media attention almost magically.

The shell had broken, and now it was time for another person to gain world prominence—a rotund, personable, much-loved pope by the name of John XXIII.

When he was elected pope in 1958, there was nothing to indicate that Cardinal Angelo Roncalli would be anything other than a caretaker pontiff, safely filling the papacy while the College of Cardinals looked for a younger, more permanent man. He was 77, he was not expected to live long, and his whole life had been so dully conformist that no one could guess the crackling bonfire of ideas that blazed secretly in his mind. Yet his term as pope utterly revolutionized Catholicism, catapulting the papacy into an office of recognized world importance. Soon after being crowned, he called the first ecumenical council in nearly a hundred years. He openly courted non-Catholics, meeting with major religious leaders from other faiths. His advice during the Cuban missile crisis evoked gratitude even from the Soviets, and his major encyclical, "Peace on Earth," won global commendation. When he died, he was one of the best loved men in the world.

Hard on the heels of John XXIII's pontificate came a new pope who chose the name Paul VI. A world traveler even before acceding to the papacy, Pope Paul undertook travels unprecedented in recent history. He went to the Middle East. He traveled to India. Soon thereafter he visited Asia, and then came to New York for an address at the United Nations. Next it was off to Portugal, and Turkey, and Colombia, to Switzerland, East Africa, Iran, Pakistan, and the Pacific. Not unexpectedly, he came to be called the "pilgrim pope." The distinctive white and yellow colors of the Vatican became familiar symbols at airports, stadiums, and churches all over the world. Ecumenism had begun in earnest, and the world began to wonder about these gentle men in pristine white, whose blessing seemed to hold thousands enthralled—men who were called vicars of Christ, and who urged the brotherhood of man and peace on earth.

Then within a few weeks two popes died, again focusing world attention on the papacy. A new pope was chosen—a dynamic, charismatic Pole who took the name John Paul II. His choice of names was not insignificant: He would combine the personal charm of John XXIII with the global travel of Paul VI. The papacy would quickly soar to prominence as one of the most influential offices in the world. The United States would even send an ambassador to the Vatican.

This much had happened in just twenty years. Meanwhile, another religious phenomenon was sweeping America, developing such power that it began to have measurable impact even in Presidential elections. It was the rise of the new religious right; to millions of people it seemed to offer the solution to America's problems.

As one looks at America today, a number of serious problems are evident: a general decline in our society; disrespect for order; a changing morality, in which diseases that are normally transmitted through sexual contact threaten even the young and innocent. Beyond this loom global dangers: the nuclear threat, a shaky world economy, acts of terrorism. Quite obviously, something is badly wrong.

At the same time an obvious fact emerges. If people would live by the most basic Biblical principles, most of our problems would greatly lessen. Many would disappear overnight.

Not surprisingly, a growing multitude of people are concluding that the solution to our world problems must be a religious one. Out of this concern has arisen a new religious-political force, determined to restore moral principles to American life. It has come to be called the new religious right, and it has had measurable impact in three Presidential elections. Its plans for the future are said to be ambitious.

Among perceptive Adventists, all this arouses no small concern, for if prophecy and history tell us anything, it is that politics and religion form the most explosive mixture in the world. But stop and analyze what is happening here. The religious right offers a whole list of ideas that in themselves are difficult to argue with. Think them through, and ask yourself which of their goals do not resonate in your own mind. This year more than 86 million crimes will be committed in America. Nearly 28 percent of all households will be touched by crime. At one time, the Federal Communications Act of 1934 prohibited the use of profanity in any broadcast, and one had to go to the theater to hear bad language or see explicit immorality. Now both are readily available on television, and one's children can be treated to a gutter environment without the inconvenience of ever leaving home.

Which of the religious right's concerns are recognizably wrong? Without the special guidance of prophecy, one could accept almost any of them as necessary solutions to problems that endanger us all.

And that illustrates a vitally important point. At the end of time, many of our gravest dangers may appear not as open challenges to liberty but as very logical attempts to

deal with real-life problems. Without the
prophecy, they might be unrecognizable. Let r
simple example.

In recent years inflation has followed a repetitive and
increasingly predictable cycle. In 1966 it began rising,
peaking in 1971 at around 6 percent. It then receded, only
to be followed by a new and higher wave in 1975, soaring
this time to well over 10 percent—double-digit inflation, a
new experience for most Americans. The wave came again
in the early 1980s, peaking at around 14 percent. By now
enough of these cycles have occurred that we can graph
them; upon doing so, one instantly sees that each new
inflationary spike has soared measurably higher than the
one before it—which leaves one wondering what implications all this may have for our future.

Some analysts have concluded that we will in fact face a
new inflationary wave, far more destructive than anything
yet seen. They may be right or wrong, but there are
certainly factors enough to justify concern—the massive
federal debt, a possible banking emergency, even the risk of
interruption in the world oil supply. Should the worst
happen, and inflation turn really catastrophic, sooner or
later government would feel compelled to intervene with
some emergency measure, such as wage and price controls.
But even that level of intervention could not subdue a
severe inflationary spike if money were in free circulation,
for market forces have a way of fueling inflation despite
government's best efforts to legislate their control. To get
the economy really in hand during a crisis, one would have
to control spending patterns almost totally. And with
today's technology, there is a temptingly easy way in which
that might be done: Get cash out of circulation and require
everyone to operate on a cashless system, where goods are
purchased by electronic fund transfer and all transactions
can be monitored by federal computers to be sure that
prices are not too high.

Actually, that would be quite simple to do. Personal
registration is virtually complete in America, through the

Social Security System. Coupled with this is an incredibly sophisticated credit card system that knows where most people are, how much they spend, whether they pay their bills. It is global in its scope: Recently I purchased some goods in a Leningrad gift shop. Not wanting to spend cash, I handed the cashier a MasterCard. He accepted it without a moment's hesitation. Walter Wriston, ex-board chairman of Citicorp, recently put it this way: "Whether we like it or not, mankind now has a completely integrated, international financial and informational marketplace capable of moving money and ideas to any place on this planet in minutes." [2]

So the transition to electronic purchasing would be no big challenge; the system necessary to do it is already essentially in place. Now visualize the United States in a time of crisis, needing to control inflation by controlling spending patterns. The solution would seem as obvious as a summer sunrise: Remove cash from circulation and require everyone to use an encoded card, by which purchases could be monitored for compliance with federal pricing regulations.

Notice something interesting here. Every step in the process we have just described is perfectly logical. Inflation crisis. Government's need to respond. An available system, already used and accepted by most Americans. A relatively minor sacrifice of personal liberty for the sake of saving the national economy. Each step in this process seems to lead logically to the next, not as an intentional assault on personal freedom but as government's honest and best effort to preserve something for its people. The process is so logical that most people might see it merely as a necessary change. Only the careful student of prophecy would discern, beneath the rhetoric and politics, beneath the nightly newscasts and the learned ramblings of editorialists, the hidden fulfillment of an ancient prophecy: "And he causeth all, both small and great, rich and poor, free and bond, to receive a mark."

Now imagine this sort of governmental power, exer-

cised at a time of crisis, when a growing majority of people
are coming to the conclusion that the nation's only hope is a
return to God. Imagine, further, that this occurs at a time
when electronic buying has rendered cash worthless, and
one is required to register in order to receive the card that is
his only source of spending power.Put the two together,
and there you have it: classic Adventist eschatology, served
up on a state-of-the-art, high-tech platter, complete with a
global information network and a stage fully set for last-day
events. Perhaps therein we get a fleeting glimpse of what
Ellen White was seeing when she warned that the time
would come when people would dump their money on the
church steps, begging that it be used, only to find it
worthless.

Perhaps therein also lies a hint of what she meant when
she said that one dollar given to God's cause now will be
worth ten dollars given later.

Perhaps, finally, we can see something of the urgency
that prompted these anguished words in 1899: "Evil angels
are constantly at work, planning their line of attack. . . .
Pray, my brethren, pray as you have never prayed before.
We are not prepared for the Lord's coming." [3]

And that leads us to the greatest question facing
Adventism today: Are we prepared? So much has happened—so much, so soon. A world military situation that
can only be called a crisis. Weapons escalating into space.
Powerful stirrings in the religious world. The equipment in
place to implement an economic interdict on those who do
not have the "mark of the beast." It all fits. Put the prophetic
profile of end-time events up against today's world, and the
two match, like two keys designed to open the same door.
Everything looks just as prophecy said it would look before
the coming of Jesus.

Everything—with one exception. One point on the
graph is still missing. "And this gospel of the kingdom shall
be preached in all the world for a witness unto all nations;
and then shall the end come" (Matt. 24:14). The final,
absolute sign of Jesus' coming remains unfulfilled. When it

does happen, the stage of history will be perfectly set. And He will come, and the war will be over, and we can go home.

Therein lies the irony. History is ready, its components faithfully assembled on stage. Heaven is ready, waiting with longing urgency to turn loose the mighty agency of the Holy Spirit. Even nonbelievers are ready—so impatiently ready that they turn to fantasy such as *Star Wars* and *E.T.* for some view of life beyond our world. Now God's people need to get ready.

And that brings up the most exciting news of all. Everything necessary to prepare the people of God for Christ's return can be accomplished in less than three years.

We know that because once in Adventism it nearly happened. We were almost ready for Jesus to come.

The story begins in 1856.

Notes

[1] Lewis Walton, *Omega*, (Washington, D.C.: Review and Herald Publishing Assn., 1981).
[2] Quoted by Michael A. Snyder in *Plain Truth*, February-March, 1985, p.21.
[3] Ellen G. White letter 201, 1899.

When Jesus Almost Came

4 It was autumn, 1856. Across the landscape of history the wind was rising—a storm wind, filled with hints of distant thunder. In young America no one seemed to be in clear control anymore; there was anger in the land, with muffled threats of oncoming civil war, and from time to time its onset glowed like heat lightning just over the horizon, crackling prophetically above places such as Charleston and Gettysburg. Soon they would become altars upon which Americans would offer 500,000 sons.

The economy, too, was headed for trouble. Just a few months hence would come the famed panic of 1857. "In the midst of all its plenty and pride," one historian wrote, "the nation woke one morning to find the glory was all a dream. While speculation was at a fever-heat and when men were wild with a mania for money-making, there came a financial crash unprecedented in the nation's history." [1]

Other problems nibbled at the fringes of history, some of them still hidden from view. At that very time Charles Darwin was polishing for publication his ideas regarding evolution. American readers of the New York *Tribune* might have noticed regular articles by a European communist named Karl Marx. And in New York Richard Gatling was busily hatching up an invention that might have been designed by the devil himself—a six-barreled gun that could fire bullets as rapidly as a man could turn its crank. It was the forerunner of the machine gun, this engine of Gatling's creation, the first in a series of new devices designed to kill with grim efficiency. In the years to come it would keep gravediggers busy.

So the autumn of 1856 was a dynamic moment, filled with events that cast long shadows into the future, as if history might be on the brink of something. And indeed, history was—something larger than most people imagined. In the autumn of this year an event occurred that would come tantilizingly close to ushering in the coming of Jesus.

It all began with an editorial in the *Review and Herald*.

On October 9, 1856, James White ran a brief article on the back page of the *Review;* it probably took most of his readers by complete surprise. Until now, Sabbathkeeping Adventists had contentedly assumed themselves to be represented by the church at Philadelphia (Rev. 3:8-11)—a congregation of brotherly love, for whom the Lord had no rebuke. But White was challenging them with a series of questions suggesting that the Laodicean message might apply to them. How well were they really doing the work of God? Were they truly represented by the era of Philadelphia, as most of them supposed? Or was there a dreadful possibility that they might actually be Laodicea—pretentious, proud of their accomplishments, but lacking in true godliness?

His questions could hardly have been more revolutionary. The roots of Adventism were still young and vital. Only twelve years had passed since the autumn of 1844, and the memories of that experience were still warm—memories of a golden moment, when thousands believed that the coming of Jesus was at hand, and revival swept the land. In the dozen years that had gone by, those who remained faithful following the Disappointment had studied intensively in the Word of God. In so doing, they had plowed squarely into one of the richest caches of truth one could imagine. The Sabbath. The judgment. The truth about death. Even an emerging understanding of health. Simultaneously they began discovering that in the Hebrew sanctuary service lay enormous insights, capable of answering some hitherto unsolved problems. For centuries theologians had been grappling unsuccessfully with a question in the Christian faith: How does one harmonize the apparent contradiction between a believer's full assurance of salvation and the possibility of later losing salvation? The brightest minds in Christianity had wrestled with that one, producing such odd inventions as purgatory, predestination, and once saved, always saved. None of their solutions had made sense, and now, in the middle 1850s, Adventists were putting the finishing touches on a system of theology that put it all together. It would come to be called the investigative judgment, and for the first time in centuries it would place the plan of salvation on a rational legal footing.

There was, in summary, much to be proud of. And as James White was about to point out, that just might be part of the problem.

As one looked at Adventism in the middle 1850s, there were multiplying signs that all was not well. A dozen years had passed, during which the believers had plumbed some of the deepest spiritual truths explored in centuries. Yet ironically, they were further from heaven than they had been in the autumn of 1844. "I was pointed back to the years 1843 and 1844. There was a spirit of consecration then that there is not now," Ellen White exclaimed in 1856. "What has come over the professed peculiar people of God?" [2]

She had said such things before. In 1852 she lamented that "many who profess to be looking for the speedy coming of Christ are becoming conformed to this world," and in 1854 she warned that "stupidity, like lethargy, seemed to hang upon the minds of most of those who profess to believe that we are having the last message." [3]

A disturbing trend was developing in Adventism. After twelve years of great discoveries, God's people were not progressing as they should spiritually. Something was wrong. One of the reasons was the editorial decision to omit references to the Spirit of Prophecy in the pages of the *Review,* to make the paper more acceptable as an evangelistic tool. As a result, fewer people listened for the prophetic voice, and fewer visions were given to Ellen White.

In late 1855 the General Conference took steps to rectify the situation, and in 1856 James White seemed to have decided to hit the crisis head-on.

"As a people we profess to believe that Christ is soon coming. Yet professed believers rush on in their worldly pursuits, taxing their entire energies in pursuit of this world as if there was no coming Jesus, no wrath of God to fall upon the shelterless, and no flaming judgment bar, where all deeds will receive a recompense. We tremble, we shudder, as we contemplate the condition of the professed people of God." [4]

"Our positions on Bible truth are clearly defined in the Scriptures, and easily defended. The present truth is so connected with the present fulfillment of prophecy that the people who read and hear our views both see and feel the force of truth. But where is a consecrated church on whom God can consistently pour out the Holy Ghost, and make them flaming instruments in giving light to the world. . . . It does not exist," he said sadly. "It cannot be found." [5]

He described mournfully how workers had "toiled over the midnight lamp" to produce tracts for Adventist witnessing, and he told how such publications "remain piled up in the office," [6] almost entirely undistributed. It would appear that in the 1850s, believers were falling into a trap that would ensnare them repeatedly in the decades ahead. God's people, immersed in the mightiest message that the imagination could conceive, were living as if the Second Coming were only a dream. They were failing to deliver the Advent message.

"O, ye Laodiceans," James White cried out, revealing himself at his evangelistic best, "our mouth is open unto you. Be not deceived as to your real condition." [7]

It was strong medicine, but it worked. Something about the fervency of his appeal resonated in the young church. Mail poured into Battle Creek from people who seem to have been just waiting for someone to raise the warning. There was God's church, trembling on the brink of the most awesome developments in human history, professing to have a judgment-hour message, yet acting as though the judgment had not come—and suddenly reality dawned, like sunrise over a scene of danger, and people began to wake up. There was nothing to be proud of—not while earth's last warning lay "piled up" in Battle Creek, undistributed by those who claimed to have God's message for the world. Adventism was not an abstract truth, to be savored in book-lined rooms, detached from the real world. Adventism was the world; it was history, and prophecy, and the two merging—merging in an ongoing drama where life and death were at issue and the destiny of souls hinged on whether believers did the work that God had given them. The final time prophecy in the Bible had occurred; now, according to Adventism, humanity would face a terminal crisis. Just ahead lay a scene of trouble so severe that the most vivid imagination could not picture it beforehand. One's only hope of survival was the coming of Jesus; nothing was as important as delivering that message.

Somehow the people of 1856 saw that. Letters poured in, by dozens, and scores, and hundreds. From Loraine, New York, one man wrote, "I am thankful that faithful brethren through whom the Lord could work have apprised us of our lukewarm state." [8] He confessed that he had been too ready to condemn others; now he took the Laodicean message for himself.

An Ohio man, who had been publicly critical of James White, wrote an open confession in the *Review:* "I have seen clearly that pride and selfishness have been mixed with all that I have done. . . . I do sincerely hope that the brethren will freely forgive me." [9] He added an interesting account of how, in response to the Laodicean message, revival and reformation were sweeping the church in the Midwest.

Nearly 350 such letters flooded the *Review* office, at a time when the total number of believers was only about two thousand. In other words, nearly 20 percent of the church responded, and without dissent they agreed that the time had come for revival. Considering the fact that each such letter no doubt represented a household, one can only conclude that a large proportion of the church was prepared to follow leadership into a new era of commitment. A revival unlike anything since 1844 began to sweep Adventism. Its extent can be sensed by the fact that even ministers felt constrained to make heartfelt, open confession.

"I have been led to consider with deep humiliation, the wrongs of my past life," wrote M. E. Cornell, a leading Adventist minister. "My example has not been right. . . . I ask the forgiveness and prayers of all I have in any way grieved. I mean to make clean work, and arise with the remnant." [10] Another pastor, A. S. Hutchins, said, "I have confessed, and still do humbly confess, my great lack of patience, my want of meekness. . . . The Lord abundantly pity and freely forgive me is my prayer." [11] With impressive force revival swept Adventism, heralded by public confession, surrender of pride, healing of differences between believers. Perhaps the mood of that moment is best summarized in a statement by James White in 1857: "The Spirit of the Lord came down upon us on Sabbath afternoon, and the Lord there plead[ed] with His people, as it were, face to face." [12]

And now another event occurred, outside Adventism in secular society, showing the extent to which happenings in the church may affect history more profoundly than we dream. In 1857 a massive revival also swept America with such power and intensity that even jaded newspaper editors put out special editions to report its progress. Historians are at a loss to explain why it occurred; it seems to have come from nowhere, arising spontaneously among laypeople in such unlikely places as the merchandising districts of New York. "In the Great Revival of 1857-1858 preaching seems to have occupied a very secondary place," one historian wrote. He explained how it "received its chief emphasis through the personal testimony of the men and women whose hearts God had touched." [13]

Ellen White once described a scene in which "servants of

God," their faces "lighted" with power, would "hasten from place to place" to proclaim the truth. [14] In 1857 the world apparently was nearly ready for just such an event, for religious interest suddenly surged everywhere. In New York, businessman Jeremiah Lanphier commenced noon prayer meetings; the idea quickly spread to Philadelphia, Boston, and other cities, until there was "scarcely a place of any considerable importance in the United States in which similar services were not undertaken." [15] In fact, it became a global phenomenon, reaching much of the English-speaking world. It came to be called a "Revival With a Million Converts." [16]

For a time it eclipsed nearly everything in the news. "Politics, casualties, crime, and the various secular interests of the day were overshadowed by the news of the revival." [17] Reporters followed it, dutifully informing their papers by telegraph of the latest events that were accompanying this wave of religious fervor. Such well-known news journals as the New York *Herald* got out extra editions, just to report its progress. "Such a time as present was never known since the days of the apostles," one journal reported. "Revivals now cover our very land, sweeping all before them, as on the day of Pentecost, exciting the earnest and simultaneous cry from thousands, What shall we do to be saved? . . . There is hardly a village or town to be found where a special divine power does not appear to be displayed." [18]

And therein lay a fascinating insight. In a way he himself only partially imagined, the writer had described something that was very real. Beyond the veil that separated the seen from the unseen world, mighty agencies were indeed in motion, hurrying between earth and heaven, going everywhere to prepare the way for God's people. We know that, because of a passage found in volume 1 of *Testimonies for the Church*. In response to revival in the church, Ellen White said, all heaven had moved into action. She described what she had seen—angels on the move, going "in every direction," working with intense activity "to prepare unbelieving hearts for the truth." [19] Before that mighty onslaught of grace, prayer meetings broke out in unexpected places. Irreligious cities were swept with revival. Laypersons handed out tracts, gave personal testimonies, held daily meetings. All this was happening outside Adventism, in secular America—in the business buildings of New York and the offices of Philadelphia, in a thousand towns and hamlets across the country. It was happening everywhere, with such intensity that even New York papers avidly reported it.

This was no accident. Heaven was arranging the stage of history for the quick completion of the third angel's message. And it was all coming as a result of revival and reformation in the church!

Then, tragically, the revival collapsed. With the stage of history set, with a depressed economy to pry people's minds away from material distractions, with angels going everywhere to prepare the way, with the nation poised on the brink of a massive civil war, with everything ready except the church, Adventism's revival withered. The bitterest irony of all was the fact that most believers had, for a time, fully expected their brief reformation to usher in the coming of Jesus.

"Nearly all believed that this message would end in the loud cry of the third angel," Ellen White wrote in 1859. [20] Yet between the dream and the fulfillment something failed. They had been near enough to the coming of Jesus to sense its presence, yet the opportunity slipped through their fingers.

So near and yet so far. Before them lay an opening so wide that it could hardly be missed—a classic end-time scenario, complete with angels preparing the way for the quick completion of the Advent message. With victory in hand, surrounded by events so providential that even secular editors accurately recognized them, God's people stumbled. From that distant era a question cries out, reaching into our own lives, begging to be answered. What went wrong? Could we make the same mistake?

On page 187 of volume 1 of the *Testimonies*, Ellen White

explains quite clearly what went wrong. "Many moved from feeling, not from principle and faith, and this solemn message stirred them. It wrought upon their feelings, and excited their fears, but did not accomplish the work which God designed that it should." They had not, she said sadly, allowed God to purify them from "their selfishness, their pride, and evil passions," and she described in chilling terms what happens when people resist the sanctifying efforts of heaven: Angels are told, "They are joined to their idols, let them alone."

For a time the Laodicean message had powerfully affected the church, healing differences, reconciling believers to each other, provoking heartfelt confession of sin. At its height the reformation was so intense that "nearly all" thought it would usher in the coming of Jesus. But the experience was superficial. They did not give the message "time to do its work"—to reach completely into their lives, producing in them the total surrender of heart that was necessary before people could stand the unimaginable challenges of the end of time. In other words, Adventists had failed in the one thing that could blunt their whole mission: They had failed to take Adventism to its ultimate.

Therein lay a sad irony, for in the middle 1850s, Adventism was developing one of the most cross-centered theologies in Christendom. For centuries Christians had looked to Calvary for relief from guilt. Three hundred years had passed since Luther had fired the Reformation with the mighty doctrine of justification by faith, and multiplied denominations now relied upon the vital truth that man's only hope is God's forgiveness. But something was missing. Too often believers acted as though Christianity began and ended with justification alone, providing them with a handy tool for relieving personal guilt but producing remarkably little benefit to the surrounding world. Believer fought believer on the battlefields of Europe, each side solemnly invoking the blessing of God on the forthcoming carnage. Too often, Christians earned no special reputation for honesty, for moral chastity, for temperance. Indeed, Muslims spurned some of the low standards in the professed Christian world, and the Chinese people suffered cruelly from the opium trade, thrust on them by professedly Christian nations.

Something was wrong, and Adventists were suggesting a solution. The power of the cross did not end with forgiveness, they said; salvation contained unlimited power, capable of transforming lives into conformity with a long-ignored standard called the law of God. For centuries Christians had used terms such as *love*, seldom bothering to translate that word into daily life. Adventism offered a concrete definition for love: Ten simple rules of life that instantly told whether love was or was not being expressed. In that clear mirror the Christian was at last without excuse for double standards and a mediocre life.

"The love of Jesus in the heart will lead to humility of life and obedience to all His commandments," Ellen White once said. "The love of Jesus that goes no farther than the lips will not save any soul, but be a great delusion." [21] Though her words seemed blunt, they were no blunter than those of John: "He that saith, I know him, and keepeth not his commandments, is a liar, and the truth is not in him" (1 John 2:4).

When one stopped to think about it, there was really no other rational way Christianity could work. One could best show love to God by treating Him as He asked to be treated—and that included worshiping Him on the day He had specified. And one could best express love to others by simply practicing the last six commandments of the Decalogue. Thus, in reemphasizing law, Adventists had unearthed a vital truth, utterly essential before Christ could return: They had found the theological basis for demonstrating what God's people would be like at the end of time. "Here is the patience of the saints," John said: "here are they that keep the commandments of God, and the faith of Jesus" (Rev. 14:12).

But all of that was only talk until a generation of God's people actually lived it. Sensing their drift from that ideal,

James White had challenged believers with the Laodicean message, and for a time revival swept the church.

"Like an electric shock the Laodicean message ran through the ranks," wrote historian Arthur W. Spaulding. "It revivified the doctrine of the sanctuary; it turned the eyes of the people from themselves to their true source of peace and power, Christ. . . . If it had had free course, it would soon have finished the gospel message in glory.

"But the work done was not thorough enough. The people generally were content with half measures. . . . They were content with a little victory. And being so content, they backslid." [22]

It was a mistake they should not have made—not in 1857. For this very year they were putting the finishing touches on a system of theology that revealed, with great clarity, just why earth's last generation would have to meet such a high standard of faith and behavior. The clue was to be found in a truth they were just now understanding in its fullness—the doctrine of the heavenly sanctuary.

For centuries theologians had been struggling with an apparent contradiction in Christian faith. On the one hand, a believer is supposed to have full assurance of salvation. "He that hath the Son hath life" (1 John 5:12), John said, pulling the future into the present. Salvation is so powerful that in its presence even time distorts. In a moment of faith, one can have the assurance that eternity begins now.

On the other hand, Jesus made it clear that not every believer would retain salvation. "He that endureth to the end, the same shall be saved" (Matt. 7:21). Therein lay the contradiction: How does one harmonize "full assurance" with continuing human free will, whereby one may actually have salvation but later decide to cast it aside? Over the centuries the best minds in Christendom had tried to solve the riddle. Calvin attempted to handle the problem at the source: Get rid of free will itself, he said, through the doctrine of predestination. Catholic theologians used another approach: Give sinners full assurance with the second chance of purgatory. Still others tried to accomplish it by getting rid of human free will at the moment of conversion so that a person could not later lose salvation by changing his mind. Thus they produced the soothing doctrine of once saved, always saved. None of the solutions made Biblical or intellectual sense.

In 1857 Adventism was formulating a system of theology that addressed that dilemma head-on, developing a model for full assurance while preserving human free will. The secret lay in the sanctuary service. The concept they offered is astonishingly similar to a commonsense mechanism used by earthly courts of law to grant someone full assurance of a legal right that cannot take place until a future time.

Let me illustrate.[23] Suppose an aggrieved spouse comes to court and proves that she is legally entitled to a divorce. In most states the law requires that the judge delay granting her a final decree, in the hope that her marriage can be mended in the meantime. Now the judge faces a dilemma: He has before him a person with an absolute legal right, but he cannot grant that right—not yet. His solution? He enters a provisional decree called an "interlocutory judgment." He writes the person's name down in the records of the court. He declares that she is entitled to a decree that will occur in the future. At the end of that time, if she still wishes final judgment entered, she is entitled to return to court and ask for it. From that moment on she has a legal right that is secure, unless she herself changes her mind. She has been given the most absolute assurance it is possible to give without robbing her of free will. Thus her probationary period ends with a conscious expression of her own will.

I recognize the dangers of trying to illustrate heavenly truths with earthly realities, and Biblical concepts with twentieth-century institutions, but here I think the analogy fits. I believe I have just described the mechanism of the plan of salvation. When a sinner comes to God in the name of Jesus, he has asserted a legal right to which even God subjects Himself—the right to live forever in His presence. It was paid for at Calvary; God willingly grants it. In the records of the heavenly court his name is entered among the redeemed—entered, in Biblical terms, in a document called the book of life. But the sinner, however repentant, remains a free moral agent, capable in the future of turning his back on salvation. Only at the end of one's probation is it possible to enter a final decree. When probation does close, that person indicates whether he still desires salvation—and he does so with the best possible evidence, "upon the record of his deeds" (Rev. 20:13, N.E.B.). Thus, every person who ever lived, saved or lost, is guaranteed a final trip to court.

Adventism was saying all this in 1857. They had even coined a term for that act: the "investigative judgment." [24]

For the first time in centuries, that doctrine put the plan of salvation on a rational legal footing. But lurking within it was a challenge of almost unimaginable proportions, and that challenge revolved around an event called the close of probation.

Throughout human history one's probation had simply closed at death. When life ceased, one's final decision had been made regarding salvation; thereafter, nothing could affect one's destiny. Thus, hidden in mankind's greatest apparent tragedy could be found one of its greatest blessings. For death gave one a final chance at salvation. Even if people had failed repeatedly in the Christian life, God's mercy could seek them one last time as death approached. Even the weakest could, in the closing glimmer of consciousness, reach out like the dying thief and grasp the hand of God. Then, before Lucifer could brew up a new agony of temptation, they could slip away into the quiet peace of death, forever secure from his devices.

In other words, for many people death was a crutch, an escape route by which they could hide at last from the possibility of failure!

Therein lies a hint of a profound truth. Everything that God allows to happen to His children, however painful, has within it an even greater blessing. In the Garden of Eden the Lord told Adam and Eve that they would "surely die." At that instant it is unlikely that they recognized it, but in reality He had given them a refuge where they could find peace at last from the nagging dangers of temptation. Without the crutch of death it is difficult to imagine how Adam could have preserved his sanity, let alone salvation, as he watched the depths to which his children would go. For him death was a moment of finality, beyond which he could rest eternally secure from the power of sin.

So it has been for the rest of the human race. Billions have lived; a vast number have undoubtedly accepted salvation. Yet in all history, we are told of only two people who didn't use the crutch of death, who transcended from this world to the next, lifted by translationary faith. Their names were Enoch and Elijah.

Enoch and Elijah—the very persons whom Ellen White says typify the people who will be living when Jesus returns! [25]

And that brings us back to Adventism. To ultimate Adventism. To the failure of 1857 and the challenge of the future. Somewhere, sometime, the crutch of death will not be available. A generation of God's people will have to face probation's close without it; and they will do so at the very end of the human genetic chain, when humanity is weakest and temptation strongest, when there is no place left to hide, and human weapons hazard the globe; when theological confusion darkens the earth, and our brightest lights go out; when former brethren become the most articulate foes of God's people. When to survive the ordeal, one will need to have the "faith of Jesus."

Probation will close while a generation of believers are still living. "He that is unjust, let him be unjust still: and he which is filthy, let him be filthy still: and he that is righteous, let him be righteous still: and he that is holy, let him be holy still. And, behold, I come quickly."

Quickly, but not yet. Jesus closes probation, but He has not yet returned. A generation of God's people is declared to be eternally redeemed while they are still in this world, still theoretically capable of turning their backs on God! Like Enoch and Elijah, they face the close of probation without having death to lean on. Here is the risk the Creator takes: He bestows salvation upon mortals who face the most dreadful conditions the world has ever seen. They must survive on faith alone.

But along with the risk comes an enormous benefit—an ultimate, clear demonstration of the power of the cross. If, through faith in Jesus, His people can come through this, then Calvary is more than a convenient mechanism for dealing with feelings of guilt. It is powerful enough to keep God's people faithful, whatever the challenge. And the universe is secure; sin will not arise again, and the war is over. Forever.

Such was the challenge of the old Advent message. Out of the sanctuary had come a new ideal for Christian living, and it was expressed in some of the most powerful language Ellen White ever used.

"Those who are living upon the earth when the intercession of Christ shall cease in the sanctuary above are to stand in the sight of a holy God without a mediator. Their robes must be spotless, their characters must be purified from sin by the blood of sprinkling. Through the grace of God and their own diligent effort they must be conquerors in the battle with evil. While the investigative judgment is going forward in heaven, while the sins of penitent believers are being removed from the sanctuary, there is to be a special work of purification, of putting away of sin, among God's people on earth. . . .

"When this work shall have been accomplished, the followers of Christ will be ready for His appearing." [26]

So that was it. In 1857 God's people had simply not finished the work of preparation necessary to meet Him. They had had revival and reformation. There had been public confession and repentance. But they had not allowed God to finish the work necessary to prepare them for the coming of Jesus. Ellen White spoke sadly of "pride, . . . fashions, . . . empty conversation, . . . selfishness." Something more was needed. They were to persevere in a "special work," a "putting away of sin." They were to be "conquerors in the battle with evil." [27] They had simply given up too soon!

"Nearly all believed that this message would end in the loud cry of the third angel," Ellen White wrote in 1859. "But as they failed to see the powerful work accomplished in a short time, many lost the effect of the message. I saw that this message would not accomplish its work in a few short months." Indeed not. It was a program that would transform their whole lives, fitting them for "the loud cry of the third angel." That would take a little time, more than a "few short months." [28]

But it could have happened much faster than most of them dreamed. In 1857, as church members began to grow weary of revival, they were—ironically—at least a third of the way into a process that could have led directly to the coming of Jesus! In fact, everything necessary to prepare them for that event could have been done if they had persevered about two more years.

On July 15, 1859, only thirty-four months after James White first published the Laodicean challenge, Mrs. White wrote that "God has given the message time to do its work." [29] It could not have been completed in a few short months, but within three years it had had "time to do its work." Time to awaken the church with a call for reformation. Time for confession of sin and unity among the believers. Time to get ready for the "loud cry of the third angel." The whole process could have been completed in a total of less than three years!

Less than three years—and God's people could have seen Pentecost. Empowered by heaven, they could have gone out into a world prepared by angels for their message. And the Civil War might never have to come, and 500,000 lives need never be lost, and, just as Ellen White said, the slaves could be liberated not by earthly conflict but by the second coming of Jesus. It could all have happened so soon.

Which brings us to the present. If the lessons of history are correct, everything necessary to prepare Adventism for the coming of Jesus can be accomplished in only three years. That means that heaven is available. It is not some far-off dream, receding before us like a mirage. It is real. We could have it. The final preparation of God's people could be completed in the lifetime of virtually everyone reading this book!

Three years. Three more winters. Three more summers. And we could be ready for something even mightier than Pentecost—the gospel flooding the world, final events forming rapidly around us, history racing toward its conclusion. "It is impossible to give any idea of the experience of the people of God who will be alive upon the earth when past woes and celestial glory will be blended," Ellen White once said. "They will walk in the light proceeding from the throne of God. By means of the angels there will be constant communication between heaven and earth." [30]

All that could be ours—all that, and heaven, too.

And that leads us to the greatest question facing Adventism today: How can we help it happen?

Notes

[1] Warren A. Candler, *Great American Revivals and the Great Republic*, pp. 189, 190, quoted in Felix A. Lorenz, *The Only Hope* (Nashville: Southern Pub. Assn., 1976), p. 53.

[2] *Testimonies*, vol. 1, p. 128.

[3] *Review and Herald*, June 10, 1852; *Early Writings*, p. 119.

[4] *Review and Herald*, Nov. 13, 1856.

[5] *Ibid.*

[6] *Ibid.*

[7] *Ibid.*, Oct. 16, 1856.

[8] *Ibid.*, Dec. 25, 1856.

[9] *Ibid.*, Feb. 26, 1857.

[10] *Ibid.*, Feb. 5, 1857.

[11] *Ibid.*, April 9, 1857.

[12] *Ibid.*, May 28, 1857.

[13] Frank G. Beardsley, *Religious Progress Through Religious Revivals*, p. 176, quoted in Lorenz, *loc. cit.*

[14] *The Great Controversy*, p. 612.

[15] Candler, *op. cit.*, p. 192, in Lorenz, *op. cit.*, p. 54.

[16] Arthur Strickland, *The Great American Revival*, pp. 132, 133, quoted in Lorenz, *loc. cit.*

[17] Beardsley, *op. cit.*, pp. 48, 49, in Lorenz, *op cit.*, p. 55.

[18] Henry C. Fish, *Handbook of Revivals*, pp. 77, 78, quoted in Lorenz, *op. cit.*, p. 55.

[19] *Testimonies*, vol. 1, p. 186.

[20] *Ibid.*

[21] Ellen G. White manuscript 26, 1885.

[22] Arthur W. Spalding, *The Origin and History of Seventh-day Adventists* (Washington, D.C.: Review and Herald Pub. Assn., 1962), vol. 2, p. 287.

[23] The following analogy was proposed in my book *Decision at the Jordan* (Washington, D.C.: Review and Herald Pub. Assn., 1982), pp. 65, 66.

[24] *Review and Herald*, Jan. 29, 1857.

[25] *Patriarchs and Prophets*, p. 89; *Prophets and Kings*, p. 227.

[26] *The Great Controversy*, p. 425.

[27] *Testimonies*, vol. 1, p. 189; *The Great Controversy*, p. 425.

[28] *Testimonies*, vol. 1, p. 186.

[29] *Ibid.*

[30] *The Faith I Live By*, p. 340.

Homeward Bound

5 Across the lengthening decades of our Adventist heritage comes a statement by Ellen White, heady with yesterday's dreams, haunting us with visions of unfulfilled tomorrows. It tells us exactly what is required to prepare a people for the coming of Jesus.

"When the character of Jesus shall be perfectly reproduced in His people, then He will come to claim them as His own." [1]

The statement is classic Adventism. Like a beacon, it flashes over the past ninety years, sometimes inspiring us, sometimes annoying us, always reminding us of the idealism of our pioneers. And if one still chooses to believe Ellen White, that statement looms into one of the greatest issues facing the church today. Will we let the life of Jesus be exhibited in us? If not, we may be in for another missed opportunity, another tragic might-have-been.

It is evident that history is forming up for something very large—so evident that even nonbelievers can feel electricity in the air. The endangered world economy. Unthinkable military peril. A rising and powerful religious movement. A system of technology fully capable of regulating commerce. We are looking at an end-time pattern; viewing it, we could make the fatal mistake of assuming that at last God is going to deliver us from this world without any special cooperation on our part.

That supposition melts instantly in the sunlight of history. Often since 1844 the stage of history has been set for the coming of Jesus . One such event we have already seen; it occurred in the middle 1850s. History was ready. The world was ready. Heaven was ready. God's people were not ready. And the golden moment vanished.

The opportunity came again about 1888 and lasted through much of the turbulent nineties. It progressed so far that national Sunday legislation was widely proposed in America. By 1899 Ellen White could see events shaping up so clearly that she cried out, "Pray, my brethren, pray as you have never prayed before. We are not prepared for the Lord's coming." [2]

There was reason for her despair. The church was about to descend into the chaos of the alpha apostasy. While the world waited, open for the quick conclusion of the gospel, God's people collapsed into introspective controversy—doctrinal disputes, heresies that struck at the very basis for Adventism, attacks on the sanctuary, the loss of some of our "brightest lights." In the process, we also lost Battle Creek Sanitarium, the flagship institution for Adventist health. Another golden moment was forfeited, and the twentieth century rolled on like an engine gone berserk, bouncing and jolting from war to depression to war again, until the sky was all alight over Hiroshima and a great terror fell over humanity.

Now another century nears its end. Once again we see a familiar pattern: history lining up, everything poised for classic Adventist eschatology, and the devil seems to have learned well how to rob us of opportunity, for we find within our own lives an all-too-familiar pattern out of yesterday's failures. Materialism. Neglect of the work of God. Worldliness. Even theological dispute over the plainest Biblical truths, while the world stands ready to hear them.

Ready for our health message—so ready that Nathan Pritiken could package basic Adventist health reform into a national success.

Ready for our clear, unashamed admission that we have had the gift of prophecy in our midst.

Ready for the one thing that could bring stability in a

decaying society: personal surrender to the law of God.

Ready for us to demonstrate in our lives what Jesus is like!

And that brings us back to one of the greatest issues facing the church today: Are we really willing to let Jesus live in us? Are we ready for ultimate, cross-centered Adventism that desires from Calvary not just relief from personal guilt, but the hope of victory?

"Higher than the highest human thought can reach is God's ideal for His children. Godliness—godlikeness—is the goal to be reached. . . .

"There is nothing that Christ desires so much as agents who will represent to the world His Spirit and character." [3]

The words ring out from old-time Adventism, describing the kind of people God needs at the end of time—able to witness effectively to a world in crisis, stable enough to face the close of probation. Their basic theology forces Adventists to accept a standard of life that is very high.

Therein comes the problem. Our experience tells us that such a standard is not easy to reach. As we search our own lives, the memory of our failures tempts us, at times, to wonder if it is possible at all. Discouraged, we might be inclined to search for a theology that offers a simpler, easier way out, something short of victory over sin.

If we'll be honest with ourselves, probably most of us have a similar story to tell: a devout Adventist upbringing, in which high standards were trumpeted at the dinner table and in the academy classroom, and we grew up visualizing ourselves as victors. If we'll continue being honest, probably in our deepest selves we resonated to that challenge. There is something about idealism that appeals to human hearts and minds. Politicians know that; John Kennedy is best remembered for his challenge to Americans to serve their country rather than be served by it. But Adventism is more than an easy slogan, to be applauded and then forgotten. It is a theology that probes our lives, constantly searching for subtle indications that we might be veering—even slightly—from a course so exact that Jesus called it the "narrow" way. Having raised the standard of God's law, we also find it to be a mirror, revealing with distressing clarity our own imperfections of character. The closer one gets to Jesus, the more clearly one sees that. And sometimes, as we fail, it is possible to become discouraged: If the Christian life is supposed to mean victory, then why do we go on sinning?

As a matter of fact, why do we sin? I can mention at least two basic reasons revealed in the Word of God: We sin either because it feels right or because it feels good. Let me illustrate.

On that fateful day in Eden when sin first entered human history, Eve found herself facing a strange and fascinating new experience. Lucifer, in the form of a familiar animal, challenged her to a process from which we are not immune even today—an intellectual exercise in which she was asked to reinterpret the word of God. "And he said unto the woman, Yea, hath God said . . . ?" (Gen. 3:1). Notice something interesting. Satan does not alarm Eve by saying that God does not exist. Nor does he awaken her to danger by saying that she never heard God speak—or, to put it in today's language, that she never read the Bible . His destruction of the word of God is much more subtle. He asks her to revise the meaning of God's word, and he gives her apparently tangible scientific evidence to prove his point. "You think that God said that there is death in this tree. Obviously He could not possibly have meant that. Look at me : I'm not dead; in fact, I have elevated to a new level of intellectual excellence. Go back, Eve, and reinterpret what God said, based on this new and better data I have given you."

Now Eve was confronted by a powerful challenge. Her outstanding mind, fresh from the hand of God, was confronted with something that intellectual honesty compelled her to admit: the existence of apparently clear evidence opposing her previous understanding of truth. Against this onslaught she had only faith to offer in rebuttal, and she failed to use it. Eve, whose genetic material could later produce an Albert Einstein, tumbled before that challenge. She sinned—because it felt "right."

Adam was soon to follow her, but for a very different reason. As he saw her coming he knew instantly where she had been — and where she was going. She was headed for a black hole called death, a horrifying, mysterious unknown from which she would never return and to which he could not accompany her, unless . . .

Unless he too indulged in the experiment of rebellion. Within him was a pain so great that one's grief at a funeral probably only partially illustrates it. He too would sin. Not because he thought it was right, but because it hurt too much not to. To put it another way, he sinned because it felt better to do so than to say No to temptation.

And the human race spiraled down into an incredible tunnel from which, without cosmic intervention, there was no escape. Something strange and supernatural enveloped their lives; like Lucifer, they tried to get more out of the system than they were able to put in—godlike status, sought by people who do not have God's life-giving power. Instead of passing on the blessings God had given them, they tried to hoard everything—and in robbing the system, they introduced a strange impostor called death.

Two sins, two reasons, the same result. One person sinned because it felt right. Another sinned because it felt good. Both were just as dead. And both died because they followed human feeling instead of an external absolute called the revealed will of God.

From that I think it is reasonable to synthesize a universal rule: When all is said and done, we sin because we choose to follow human feeling instead of principle.

A few months ago I was in my airplane over central California. It had been a stormy evening, and now night darkened the world, giving me only a dim horizon of scattered city lights far below. The ragged remnants of a spring storm were still strewn across the sky, and from time to time I flew into a cloud. There was no warning; the windscreen just suddenly went blank, blotting out my view of the outside world. Immediately my eyes darted to the instrument panel—nine glowing circles that told me whether I was on course, level, and in control.

In aviation there is a widely recognized problem called vertigo, a condition that can pester pilots when they lose their view of the horizon. Unable to supplement his or her sense of balance with visual cues, a pilot can quickly lose any idea of which way is up. The result generally is a deadly, descending turn called a graveyard spiral.

So my eyes went hungrily to the panel, searching the instruments, demanding input as to how well I was flying. Was I still level? Was I headed in the right direction? Was I maintaining altitude? Suddenly a thought swept over me—how very much my instruments are like the law of God! A few meters, probing every facet of my flight, telling me whether I am flying safely. A few simple rules, searching my life, telling me whether I am spiritually right. The greater my experience as a pilot, the more quickly I recognize the first indications of trouble—and I take the warnings from the instruments not with resentment but with gratitude. They are my link with life. And the closer I get to Jesus, the quicker the law will reveal my imperfections of character.

But do I welcome that input? Or do I resent it, not wanting feedback on the quality of my life?

Isn't it strange, I thought: A pilot cries out for data, begging to be told where he might improve. The loss of even one vital instrument can cause a memorable jolt of adrenalin. But how often Christians try to ignore the instrument panel, following feeling instead of an external absolute that can lead them safely home. In the air we demand data that is often critical of our performance. In life, we too frequently reject it.

So it seems reasonable to say that if we are to address the problem of sin successfully, we must first recognize the nature of our enemy and why we so often fail. I believe that failure enters our lives when we allow our actions to be governed by inclination rather than principle. If that is so, then a basic step in victorious Christian living is a conscious act of the will: a decision to dethrone feeling and to replace it with something better—an external absolute called the will of God. And here Adventism offers the Christian one of its monumental insights, filled both with challenge and promise. That external absolute is God's law—all ten instruments, not just nine!

But if we stopped there and said no more, we would find ourselves in an agony of failure brilliantly described by Paul in Romans 7. "For I delight in the law of God after the inward man: but I see another law in my members, warring against the law of my mind. . . . O wretched man that I am! who shall deliver me from the body of this death?" Paul had an answer, and it was outside himself: "I thank God through Jesus Christ our Lord." (verses 22-25). He found in Jesus the solution to the impossible problem, and then he went on to the mighty song of victory found in Romans 8: "For what the law could not do, in that it was weak through the flesh, God sending his own Son . . . condemned sin in the flesh: that the righteousness of the law might be fulfilled in us, who walk not after the flesh, but after the Spirit" (verses 3, 4).

In other words, once we have identified the problem, we must hand it off to the same source needed by Paul. We human beings are adept at seeing issues clearly and yet steering crookedly; human feeling must be dethroned, but if we tackle that giant on our own, we are doomed to a life of frustration, in which God's law looms like an ever-receding rainbow, beautiful but unattainable, mocking our dreams, leading us at last to such discouragement that we might give up altogether. To overcome, we must not only identify our problem; we must learn the vital lesson of surrender. The most graphic illustration of that process is found in an event in the life of Jesus.

In earthly time it possibly occurred a few months prior to 4 B.C., but the incident we are about to describe did not take place on earth. It happened in the cosmos, eons distant, probably in the center of the universe. Two Beings were in conversation, infinitely powerful Beings, from whom flowed an endless stream of fiery light, as if love itself began here, going outward into all creation. They were coequal. They had life inherent within Them, and They were unlimited by either time or space. Each had the power of creation.

Yet as One spoke, His words sounded strangely like those of a man. He was giving up a part of Himself—surrendering His will to the other! The whole awesome story can be found in two places in the Bible, Psalm 40 and Hebrews 10. "Wherefore when he cometh into the world, he saith, Sacrifice and offering thou wouldest not, but a body hast thou prepared me" (Heb. 10:5). In other words, you are listening to the last conversation between Father and Son before the Son left infinity and spiraled downward into a human cell. The time had come. It was the moment to say Goodbye, and the words go on, so deep with meaning that the human mind bends before them. "Lo, I come (in the volume of the book it is written of me,) to do thy will, O God" (verse 7).

To do Thy will. Infinite Deity was giving up something. A member of the Godhead was surrendering to another member. When He faced sin as a man, it would not be in His own power. He would do the will of His Father.

Nine earthly months go by, and the first sensation He feels on earth is probably the straw of a Bethlehem manger, poking through His little blanket. There are curious sensations; when the sky gets dark the air grows chilly in the stable, and a lamp is lit that gives a flickering light. From time to time strange faces peer over the edge of the manger—a few humble-looking men with oily hands and lint on their clothes; a few others, dressed in finery, whose faces bear an odd mixture of reverence and curiosity.

One night He senses commotion: The little family gets up suddenly and goes out into the predawn blackness, headed for the flat land with the great river and the odd stone mountains. Jesus, the Majesty of heaven, is growing up as a little boy.

74

And He never sins, not even as a child. Why? There is more to it than a good home influence or a godly mother. Much more. The mystery of salvation is being acted out—the same salvation by which His children will overcome. He does not sin, because He has surrendered His will to a loving heavenly Father. "Thy will be done." In the hardest hours of His sad visit to this world that principle will never be broken. And thus He lives without sin.

Thirty years go by, and He begins to preach—not pompous sermons but simple stories out of life that touch the heart and plumb the mind. In the Temple at Jerusalem one can hear three theories about anything. Some believe there is a resurrection; some don't. Probably others aren't sure who is right. Learned men in Alexandrian robes argue in polysyllabic terms on street corners over issues that don't even exist, while God's people starve for the simple proclamation of truth. And suddenly, there is this young Galilean rabbi who tells about salvation in language that reaches the soul, and they come by thousands to hear Him.

Among the crowd is a Pharisee, a Jewish lawyer, who senses that here might be the answer to life's dilemma. One night he finds the Lord and asks Him about eternal life. Jesus goes right to the heart of everyone's problem: Nicodemus, your trouble is simply that you came into the world the wrong way. You were born with the heritage of Adam and Eve, who tried to get more out of the system than they put in. Go back and reenter the world the way I did, absolute surrender of self to a loving heavenly Father. It is a new beginning, so complete that it can be called being "born again."

Nicodemus is trained in law. He is adept at argument, and he sees what he takes to be a flaw in Christ's statement. Go back? How can anyone go back? Our whole lives are a series of decisions that bind us to ever-narrowing options, so that our futures are often ruled by our past mistakes . What about my sad yesterdays? How can I begin again?

Jesus' answer to that question is found in John 3:16. It is the gospel. It is the third angel's message in verity. It is

Adventism. It is what being a Christian is all about. Nicodemus, that is why I am here. I know about your yesterdays. I have the best bargain in the world for you: Give Me your yesterdays, and I'll give you Mine.

Thus you are free, and the past has no right to shackle you; that is a beginning so complete that seven times in sin, Mary Magdalene can rise again, with no past to accuse her. It is full assurance at its ultimate, with obedience born not of legalism but of love.

Another vital step in overcoming sin is thus the simple lesson of surrender. And that brings us to one of the most practical questions in Christianity today: How? How, in practical daily living, does one "surrender" to God?

The world is filled with Christians who, each in his own way, use terms like *surrender*. Ask any Christian, and he or she would probably say something about surrendering one's heart "to the Lord." But what do they mean by that? How does one do it?

Once again, I believe that Adventism provides the clearest answer, and for a very simple reason: Adventism accepts the entire law of God, without attempting to rewrite the fourth commandment to suit human tradition or convenience. Go any distance short of that, and you can speak about surrender all you wish, but you haven't really done it. You have refused to surrender on the one point that identifies God as sovereign. And having introduced that reservation into your theology, you are incapable of speaking consistently about surrender at all.

So Adventism offers yet another clear answer to a practical Christian problem: Surrender is accomplished, in the daily life, by unqualified acceptance of God's will. Even when it costs us something. Even when we cannot validate His request with human reason, and the rule seems strangely arbitrary.

Such as a day of worship.

Or a tree in Eden.

We obey even when we cannot understand why. Thus, in the absolute acceptance of His law, we are actually surrendering human will. In the process, Satan is robbed of the means by which he causes us to sin! "Pure religion has to do with the will," Ellen White wrote. She explained that at the Fall, human will was "given into the control of Satan." By man's transgression an alien force had gained legal title to the will, where all decisions are made regarding conduct. Without cosmic intervention humanity would be a race of slaves. That, she declared, was one of the major issues at Calvary. Christ died to repurchase the human will. And it is through the will that one sins or overcomes!

Look at the *Index to the Writings of Ellen G. White* and you will be astonished at the wide implications connected with the will: Yielding to temptation is an act of will. Angels are unable to control one's mind against his will. Even blood perfusion in the vascular system is affected by the will! Whether one lives or dies is governed by that mysterious power of the human mind, purchased at Calvary.

"You will be in constant peril until you understand the true force of the will," Ellen White once wrote to a discouraged young man who had a sad history of good intentions but repeated failures. "You may believe and promise all things, but your promises or your faith are of no value unless you put your will on the side of faith and action. . . . Your feelings, your impressions, your emotions, are not to be trusted, for they are not reliable," she continued, using language that reminds one of the pilot blinded by clouds. "But you need not despair. . . . You cannot control your impulses, your emotions, as you may desire, but you can control the will." [4]

"It is for you to yield up your will to the will of Jesus Christ; and as you do this, God will immediately take possession, and work in you to will and to do of His good pleasure." [5]

In other words, one surrenders to Jesus through the mechanism of the will! Once again, I find an illuminating example of this in the world of flight.

I am on an instrument approach to Los Angeles International Airport. I am wrapped in a thick layer of coastal clouds, so I cannot see the San Gabriel Mountains, but I know that they are somewhere to my left, rising three thousand feet above my present altitude. If I make a mistake and veer in that direction, I will have only three minutes before impacting one of the hidden summits. Ahead of me is a 747; behind me, in trail, is a DC-10. To my right, a United 727 is circling for its final approach. Somewhere beneath me is a helicopter. I cannot see any of them; they are revealed to me by a radar controller on the ground, who alone can penetrate the fog and guide me safely to a landing. At that moment the radio crackles with my call sign: "November Three Three Delta, you are cleared for the approach, Runway 24 Left. Turn right, heading 230 degrees, maintain 150 knots ."

Every fiber of my being is at work—hands, feet, eyes, ears. This is for real; a mistake here could be much more than an embarrassment or inconvenience. Life itself is at stake, and I put everything I have into the effort. The compass wanders two degrees left; I bring it back. The glide slope receiver comes to life, following an invisible beam that tells me whether I am too high or too low; I watch it hungrily. As the instructions come over the radio, I acknowledge them immediately, telling the air traffic controller that I will follow her directions.

In years of flying I have noticed something interesting. When a pilot replies that he will obey his landing instructions, I have never heard another pilot come on the frequency and say, "Legalist! What are you trying to do, work your way to the ground?"

Notice something else. I am still flying the airplane. The radar controller does not reach up through space, seizing the control yoke and the throttles. I manipulate the controls, adjust power, scan the instrument panel. The custodial details of putting the airplane on the ground remain mine to do. What, then, have I given up as I follow orders to a safe landing? My will. I have surrendered my will to someone who can see more clearly than I can.

And that, too, is the Christian life. At the Fall, Adam and

Eve lost their spiritual horizon. The fog of sin wrapped around the windscreen, and we are now endangered by the instability of human feeling. Surrounding us are multiplied dangers we cannot even see. For that reason God sends us instructions regarding the dangers, steering us toward safety. The channel through which they come is called prophecy.

But surrendering our wills to Him does not imply that we have ceased to be involved with practical Christian living. Like the pilot, there is much for us to do. God gives us the Sabbath. His grace enables us to keep it. But, as Mervyn Maxwell has so graphically said, it is we who mop the floors and vacuum the carpets, who cook the food on Friday as we get ready for God's special day. Angels do not sew on missing buttons or write our sad letters of apology, nor does God's grace buy the literature with which to share our faith. Hebrews 11:7 says that Noah "became heir of the righteousness which is by faith" when, believing God's warning about the Flood, he "prepared an ark to the saving of his house." Belief alone would have earned him neither salvation nor protection if he had kept it at the level of mere mental assent. He needed to express his faith in works as well as in words. And so do we.

That, however, does not imply that doing right is necessarily easy. We speak glibly about Noah, safely insulated by the passage of five thousand years from the brutal ridicule, the bankrupting cost, the seemingly endless decades of work. To endure that for 120 years simply for the sake of faith is a classic example of true surrender; everything on the line—his whole future, his reputation, even his personal wealth—in exchange for something he couldn't even scientifically prove. There is nothing easy about such an experience.

In his own unique way Paul described the process of Christian surrender as crucifixion, and his illustration is rich with meaning. A person being crucified did not die quickly; day after day passed in which he was immobilized but conscious, fully able to cry out in pain, to beg to be taken down from the cross. So it is with us. Day after day duty collides with inclination, self cries out to be liberated. The only way to win a fight like that is to immerse one's self in the Word of God, to slam shut every avenue by which Satan can gain access to one's selfish inclinations, to spend a "thoughtful hour each day" looking at Jesus, to take one's new, growing faith and strengthen it by witnessing to others.

A few months ago I was giving a radio interview on an Adventist college station. When we went off the air I explained some of this to the announcer, telling him that I thought one of man's major roles in salvation was simply to ignore the pleas of crucified self. "That may be,"he replied, "but I have found that to be hard—very, very hard."

Well, whoever said anything about its being easy? People have burned to death for this faith. Joseph went to prison for it—when, with a little rationalization, he could have convinced himself that Potiphar's wife was just a human being to whom he should show "love." Daniel risked death for it, and so did his three friends; and so, for that matter, did Jeremiah and John, Stephen and Peter, Huss and Jerome, Martin Luther. "And what more shall I say? for the time would fail me to tell of Gedeon, and of Barak, and of Samson, and of Jephthae; of David also, and Samuel, and of the prophets: who through faith subdued kingdoms, wrought righteousness, obtained promises, stopped the mouths of lions, quenched the violence of fire, escaped the edge of the sword, out of weakness were made strong, waxed valiant in fight" (Heb. 11:32-34).

"These all died in faith, not having received the promises, but having seen them afar off, . . . embraced them, and confessed that they were strangers and pilgrims on the earth" (verse 13). Nowhere therein is it suggested that the gospel is easy. But the language in Hebrews seethes with power, telling us that salvation is possible. Possible through faith—a faith that works.

What kind of faith will it take to finish the work of God? The same kind of faith that was seen at its beginning.

It is a spring day, and the horror of the crucifixion is past. Jesus has come forth from the grave with the mighty statement "I am the resurrection, and the life." Now, with a few close friends who have shared His life on earth, He is trudging up a rocky hillside.

All around them are reminders of the lessons He has given. A vine, to illustrate the close relationship between man and God. A lily, to show the beauty of simplicity. A little brown sparrow, whose fate will not escape His notice, even from the throne. For the rest of their lives, their minds will swirl with memories—the way He held the children that day, the way He prayed . . .

And suddenly Jesus is leaving them, drawn upward by a force even stronger than earthly love. Perhaps they should have known that this would come, but there was really no way to prepare for it—no easy way to say Goodbye to Someone who means more than life; and for long minutes they stand transfixed, numbed by it all, lost in wonder. Three and a half years in the presence of God, and now it is over.

Over . . . but not really. A great thought fills their minds. The same Man who toiled with them up the stony road to Bethany, who had eaten breakfast with them that morning and given them a last Goodbye, has gone to share His Father's throne.

Now the future opens like a spring horizon. They have a Friend at the throne! Their faith soars higher and higher until it grasps the mightiest argument anyone could offer: "Who would dare to accuse us? . . . Only Christ Jesus, and Christ died for us, Christ also rose for us, Christ reigns in power for us, Christ prays for us!" (Rom. 8:33, 34, Phillips). Vitalized by that faith, there is nothing they cannot do, no challenge they cannot endure. Only a few days are required to bring them "all with one accord in one place." The Holy Spirit possesses them, and—significantly—they immediately enter into another heaven-ordained process by which one gains strength to overcome: They begin witnessing to others!

A-6

81

Ellen White once put it this way: "Strength to resist evil is best gained by aggressive service." [6] By taking the war to the enemy, by seeking to rescue others from the power of sin, we ourselves are strengthened to overcome it! Can failing to follow through in that area be still another reason why we sometimes find victory difficult?

A Friend at the throne. Someday we too will grasp the implications of that truth. Jesus is real. There is no spiritual gift we cannot have in response to faith. "Ask, then; ask, and ye shall receive." [7] "For the pardon of sin, for the Holy Spirit, for a Christlike temper, for wisdom and strength to do His work, for any gift that He has promised, we may ask; then we are to believe that we receive, and return thanks to God that we have received." True, it may not come just in the way we expect, but it will come in the way and at the time "when we need it most." [8]

Someday that will happen within Adventism. Pentecost will be repeated, and the world will quickly hear the Advent message. "The great work of the gospel is not to close with less manifestation of the power of God than marked its opening. . . . Servants of God, with their faces lighted up and shining with holy consecration, will hasten from place to place to proclaim the message from heaven. By thousands of voices, all over the earth, the warning will be given. Miracles will be wrought, the sick will be healed, and signs and wonders will follow the believers." [9]

When that occurs, the last obstacle to the coming of Christ will have passed. Empowered by the faith of Jesus, God's people will be ready to meet Him. And we will be homeward bound.

Homeward bound! Out through the glorious interstellar clouds of Orion, glowing with shades of neon green and scarlet. Out beyond the limits of imagination, to a place that even prophets have struggled to describe. A throne is there, and from it flows a river of fiery light. There the angels walk on a glittering pavement called the "stones of fire." As the redeemed enter the city, angels will form up in two lines, a living corridor, watching in wonder as God's people pass between them—earth's survivors, coming home.

"There, immortal minds will contemplate with never-failing delight the wonders of creative power, the mysteries of redeeming love. . . . There the grandest enterprises may be carried forward, the loftiest aspirations reached, the highest ambitions realized; and still there will arise new heights to surmount, new wonders to admire, new truths to comprehend, fresh objects to call forth the powers of mind and soul and body." [10]

"There are ever-flowing streams, clear as crystal, and beside them waving trees cast their shadows upon the paths prepared for the ransomed of the Lord. There the wide-spreading plains swell into hills of beauty, and the mountains of God rear their lofty summits. On those peaceful plains, beside those living streams, God's people, so long pilgrims and wanderers, shall find a home." [11]

Heaven is real. Heaven is within reach. And I think it is time to go there. For nearly 150 years Adventists have dreamed of that place; 150 years is too long to wait. Let us arise and go. It is a goodly land, and we are well able to go up and possess it.

Robert F. Kennedy made famous this quote: "Some people see things as they are, and ask, Why? I dream of things that never were, and ask, Why not?"

Indeed, why not?

Why not heaven?

Why not us?

Why not now?

Notes

[1] *Christ's Object Lessons*, p. 69.
[2] Ellen G. White letter 201, 1899.
[3] *Messages to Young People*, p. 40.
[4] *Ibid.*, pp. 151, 152.
[5] *Ibid.*, p. 151.
[6] *The Acts of the Apostles*, p. 105.
[7] *Messages to Young People*, p. 250.

ADVENT!

[8] *Education*, p. 258.
[9] *The Great Controversy*, pp. 611, 612.
[10] *Ibid.*, p. 677.
[11] *Ibid.*, p. 675.

There Has Been
a Voice Among Us

6 It was Sunday; the atmosphere was electric. In the narrow streets of Jersualem, news crackled from person to person, sending ripples of excitement across the city. "He's done it! The Messiah has made His move! It looks as if He will try for the throne. He's coming—from somewhere out toward Bethany !"

This was news that the religious leaders had been dreading. They had half expected something like this, wondering for months when the Galilean teacher would challenge them openly for power. Now, jolted by the tidings, they hurried up the Bethany road, faces furrowed with concern, robes flapping.

There was reason enough for them to worry. In Jerusalem, normally crowded by Passover visitors, the trumpet call for evening sacrifice brought only a handful of people to the Temple. "The world has gone after Him," they exclaimed despairingly. They were not at all reassured to learn that for the first time anyone could remember, He was not walking; He was riding—a mode of entry traditionally reserved for kings. [1]

So this was it. He had chosen the Passover time to try it, when Jews from all over the world would be present—a brilliant move, one that, had their roles been reversed, they themselves would have used. Now it was live or die. They would have to silence Him, whatever the risk. And the risk might not be too bad: People were notoriously fickle. If the leaders could arrange for a crucifixion, the shame and stigma of His death would probably quell most of His popular support. At any rate, it was vital to try.

The procession was approaching Jerusalem, growing as it came, a colorful splash on the overlooking hillside. If the rulers were worried, no one else seemed to be; no one could remember such open joy. If this meant what it seemed to mean, then the days of Roman occupation were over. The dream would come at last—Israel the queen, ruled by Messiah Himself, wealthy and blessed, the envy of the world.

It was like the triumphal return of a conquering army, but no victory procession had ever been like this. There were no mourning captives, marching in chains; no supply wagons loaded with plundered wealth. Instead, the crowd seemed to be composed of people who had been set free: blind men who had received their sight, cripples who could walk, children who had learned that even the King Himself had time—and a lap—for the world's little people. Most impressive of all, the procession was led by a man who had once been quite dead—four days dead, so very dead that his sister had not wanted to open the grave, even at the request of Jesus. Now he was alive again. It was beyond imagining, yet it had happened: ultimate, absolute proof that the Man who approached the scowling line of Jewish leaders was God Himself, the I AM out of the seventh day of Creation.

"Master," they stormed, "rebuke thy disciples" (Luke 19:39).

Beyond the crowd, beneath the low crest of Olivet, the city of Jerusalem stretched away into the setting sun. At the northeast corner stood the Temple, primal wonder of the world, wrapped in snowy marble and embellished with gold. Even Rome stood in awe of this building, where from time to time the visible presence of Deity had seemed to hover. For more than a thousand years Jerusalem had been the place where God had tried to bring about a glorious dream: Israel, the witness to the world, holy, healthy, happy, safe within the protection of God's law, hallowed by the promise of the world's Redeemer . Here Solomon had reigned in the brief glory days, when the dream had shown hints of fulfillment: all the world calling, awestruck at the wisdom of a people led by God Himself. Here, within the very presence of divine love, Israel had repeatedly gone shipwreck on the reef of sin. And here the prophets had given their solemn warnings, begging God's people to reform before it was too late.

The prophets—so many prophets. Jeremiah. Faithful Zacharias, who had been slain in the temple court, and whose blood still visibly stained the pavement. Ezekiel, who had cried out for reformation. Isaiah, whose words, uncomprehended by spiritual leaders, foretold a suffering Messiah. They had rejected them all, and now they were rejecting the One who had sent the prophets to them. The dream was dying, and the Son of God began to cry, "O Jerusalem, Jerusalem, thou that killest the prophets, . . . how often would I have gathered thy children together, even as a hen gathereth her chickens under her wings, and ye would not!" (Matt. 23:37).

It was sunset over Jerusalem; the day was ending, and with it, a city's probation. "When the fast westering sun should pass from sight in the heavens, Jerusalem's day of grace would be ended. While the procession was halting on the brow of Olivet, it was not yet too late for Jerusalem to repent. The angel of mercy was then folding her wings to step down from the golden throne to give place to justice and swift-coming judgment. But Christ's great heart of love still pleaded for Jerusalem. . . . While the last rays of the setting sun were lingering on Temple, tower, and pinnacle, would not some good angel lead her to the Saviour's love, and avert her doom? Beautiful and unholy city, that had stoned the prophets, that had rejected the Son of God, that was locking herself by impenitence in fetters of bondage— her day of mercy was almost spent!" [2]

Mercy's last call had been made, and the reply came fast and hard: "Master, rebuke thy disciples."

Soon two paths would diverge. The Son of God, His mission on earth completed, would go out into the cosmos, on and on somewhere beyond infinity, where unfallen beings waited to welcome Him home. And on earth, Jerusalem would follow its own path into deepening terror.

More than thirty years go by. Desperate for the national liberty that they thought the Messiah would bring, the Jews revolt against Rome. On Calvary, crosses spring up as thick as forest trees. In the fateful spring of A.D. 70, Rome's General Titus lays siege to Jerusalem—even as rival Jewish factions inside fight bloody battles among themselves. From Mount Scopus, the Twelfth and Fifteenth Roman legions hammer down, joining the Tenth Legion from Jericho. Out west, near Emmaus, the battle-hardened troops of the Fifth Legion march eastward, following a road once walked by Jesus and His two wondering disciples. Roman armies smash through the city's western defenses, penetrating part of Jerusalem. And then, encountering resistance in the central city, they throw a siege dike around it—a continuous line of defense, every inch of it guarded by alert soldiers, so no one can escape. For those inside, it will be a fight to the death.

"O Jerusalem, Jerusalem, thou that killest the prophets." There had been a voice among them, and they would not listen.

And there has been a voice among us. For more than seventy years it tarried in our midst, telling us of events beyond the realm of mortal sight—of angels hurrying between heaven and earth, of a great cosmic controversy, of the lovely Jesus. There was life in that voice; we are constantly reminded of that, as science continues to confirm what we were told a hundred years ago. We have had in our midst the gift of prophecy.

As was so often the case in the past, it came through someone whom only God would have chosen—a young woman of 17, whose humble background and limited education seemed to destine her for obscurity. But one day late in 1844 the curtain parted and she saw a great spiritual truth. There was a path, she said, that stretched from earth to heaven. Each step along that path carried one ever higher; with each step the people of God would learn to depend less on self and more on Him. It was the path of faith.

For a long lifetime she never varied from that vision. We have two great tasks, she said: to prepare for the coming of Jesus, and to prepare the world. And in simple faith, a handful of believers began to act on that dream.

There was no way they could do what she described—not to human appearances—but they would try. They went out in horse-drawn wagons and open sleighs, in wood-burning trains and sailing ships, not knowing how such a few people could warn the world, but trusting that if that was their mission, they would at least begin. They didn't stop until the flag of the message was planted in Europe and Asia, in the thin, cold air of the Andes and on the black sand beaches of Tahiti, in Russia and the continent of Africa. The task seemed impossible, but they began.

And always that voice was urging them on, telling them that one's best could become something even better. We needed schools, so that Adventist young people could learn from teachers who loved the old Advent message. We needed hospitals, both to heal and to witness. We needed publishing houses. We even needed to be able to train physicians, so they could become medical evangelists. Fired by faith, we found there was nothing we couldn't do—and we did it all.

Everything, except the greatest dream of all—reflecting Jesus so fully in our lives that all the world could see what He is like. We tried, and sometimes, as in 1856, the dream seemed near enough to touch. But 150 years have passed, and we are still here; and some people today have begun to wonder if it was ever possible.

We may wonder, but Ellen White never did. For she had seen the future of Adventism—a future that has still to be written. It came in a vision on November 20, 1857, and it portrayed God's plan for a victorious church, right up through the return of Christ.

She viewed the "people of God." They were separated

into two groups, one of which was praying earnestly—"with strong faith and agonizing cries . . . pleading with God." The second group also claimed to be people of God, but there was a difference. They "did not participate in this work of agonizing and pleading. They seemed indifferent and careless," and did not resist an atmosphere of "thick darkness" brought on by evil angels, crowding around them in an effort to blind the church. "They were not resisting the darkness," she said. "The angels of God left these, and I saw them hastening to the assistance of those who were struggling with all their energies to resist the evil angels." Soon she "lost sight" of those who did not pray.[3]

"I asked the meaning of the shaking I had seen, and was shown that it would be caused by the straight testimony called forth by the counsel of the True Witness to the Laodiceans. . . . Some will not bear this straight testimony. They will rise up against it, and this will cause a shaking among God's people." [4]

But the vision did not end there. Once again she saw those who had been in such earnest prayer. "Said the angel: 'Look ye!' My attention was then turned to the company I had seen, who were mightily shaken. I was shown those whom I had before seen weeping and praying with agony of spirit. The company of guardian angels around them had been doubled." [5]

The force of that statement comes into perspective when one remembers that one night a single angel overflew the Assyrian army camp, and 185,000 battle-ready soldiers died. That is the sort of protective power we are speaking of—and for the people of God who earnestly pray, such protection is doubled. Small wonder, then, what Ellen White saw next. The saints were marching "in exact order, firmly, like a company of soldiers." No confusion over which direction they should go, no divisive controversy over theology, no wondering if the Advent message was correct. Like the apostles at Pentecost, they were "all with one accord in one place"—soldiers of the cross, going out to accomplish their mission at last. Their faces, though marked by the ordeal of the shaking, now "shone with the light and glory of heaven." [6]

"The numbers of this company had been lessened. Some had been shaken out, and left by the way. The careless and indifferent, who did not join with those who prized victory and salvation enough to perseveringly plead and agonize for it . . . were left behind in darkness, but their numbers were immediately made up by others taking hold of the truth and coming into the ranks." [7]

How vivid a description that is of our present world! When I was in college in the early sixties, it was not all that hard to walk away from Adventism. Newport Beach, Palm Springs, and Hollywood Boulevard were only an hour's drive away. John Kennedy was in the White House, and about all we had to do to get Russian missiles out of Cuba was to tell Khrushchev to move them. In those days one could grow careless in the Christian life without too many warning signals from history.

Today, that is not so easy to do. When one opens the door to leave Adventism, he encounters a globe in crisis. One no longer tells the Russians what to do; in the past twenty-five years they have amassed nearly four times the nuclear throw weight of the United States. The economy gives off weird creaks and groans, like a tired building about to do something destructive to itself, and Hollywood Boulevard is sheathed in an acrid layer of smog. As one opens the door of the church to walk away, more likely than not he will encounter two or three people on the outside, looking in with interest and saying, "What's in there? Is it better than what we have? We don't like it very much out here."

Standing at that door, a nominal Adventist would face a conflicting swirl of emotions—discomfort with the church, fear of leaving it. Confronted by such a dilemma, he would be powerfully tempted to resolve it by creating some way of remaining in Adventism while avoiding its challenging standards—a new theology, for example, that allows one to accept a lowered standard while claiming to be redeemed.

And if anyone—including Ellen White—upset that delicate psychological adjustment by reminding him that he was wrong, he might become quite angry.

So the vision disclosed a shaking, in which some left Adventism and others took their places. But through it all the work triumphed. God's people witnessed to the world "in great power." She asked what had made such a change in the church, and her accompanying angel replied, "It is the latter rain, the refreshing from the presence of the Lord, the loud cry of the third angel." [8]

So that is it! The latter rain and the shaking. The shaking results from resistance to the True Witness to Laodicea. The True Witness is the voice of God, expressed through the gift of prophecy. And we have had that voice among us! To finish the work, we must first get our hearts and minds back into the truth God has given us—not just casually, but intensively, as if life itself depends upon it. When we do, acting in faith upon the truth we read, everything will fall into place, even the elusive dream, victorious Christian living.

The vision continued, moving rapidly. Unbelievers, shaken by the powerful message of God's people, "were all astir. The zeal and power with the people of God had aroused and enraged them. Confusion, confusion, was on every side." [9] History raced rapidly into end-time events—a world in crisis, civil measures taken against believers, constant prayer that continued through day and night. The vision does not describe the precise problems God's people endure, but they are so severe that onlooking angels have to be restrained from going prematurely to their rescue. It is the time of Jacob's trouble, and the believers endure by faith alone.

"Soon I heard the voice of God which shook the heavens and the earth. There was a mighty earthquake. . . . Jesus was seen in the clouds of heaven, and the faithful, tried company were changed in a moment, in the twinkling of an eye, from glory to glory. The graves were opened and the saints came forth, clothed with immortality, crying: 'Victory over death and the grave!' " [10] Revival and reformation, a deep seeking after God, had at last prepared God's people for the Second Coming. Now they could go home.

That is Adventism—victorious Adventism, the only sort of Adventism that has any meaning in our world. It is our heritage. If we would let it, it could happen to us. We could be that generation.

For nearly a century and a half we have dreamed that dream, longed for its fulfillment, waited and wondered. Now we have a golden moment in which to make it happen. Everything in history that must occur before the coming of Jesus has either already taken place or is lined up for speedy fulfillment. Even the hard task of warning 4 billion people has been handed to us on an electronic platter, in the form of communication satellites that can relay news simultaneously to the entire globe. I am convinced that some of our most effective witnessing at the end of time will be on prime time evening news—given to us absolutely free, simply because we have become a global issue. If that is so, then we already have the hardware necessary to warn the globe in a matter of weeks!

A brief time of spiritual preparation. History waiting, all ready for its last rapid events. Even the communication equipment in place to reach the entire world. How quickly we could be home!

Once, there was a voice among us. For seventy years she begged people to get ready for the coming of Jesus. Often she was disappointed. Once, grieving over how carelessly God's people treated His counsel to them, she wrote, "I seldom weep, but now I find my eyes blinded with tears; they are falling upon my paper as I write." [11] And she openly wondered how much longer we could expect the gift of prophecy to continue when we didn't follow the light we already had. But she never gave up.

She was often disappointed, but she *never gave up*. Not on Adventism. Not on us. Somewhere, sometime, a generation of believers would make it happen. Jesus would come.

Across the long, shadow-filled decades, the words still come, as clear and poignant as they were in 1900:

"Brethren, to whom the truths of God's word have been opened, what part will you act in the closing scenes of this world's history? Are you awake to these solemn realities? Do you realize the grand work of preparation that is going on in heaven and on earth? . . . Let none now tamper with sin, the source of every misery in our world. . . . Let not the destiny of your soul hang on an uncertainty." [12]

"If you neglect or treat with indifference the warnings that God has given, if you cherish or excuse sin, you are sealing your soul's destiny . . .

"Could the curtain be rolled back, could you discern the purposes of God and the judgments that are about to fall upon a doomed world, could you see your own attitude, you would fear and tremble for your own souls and for the souls of your fellow men. Earnest prayers . . . would go up to heaven . . .

" 'Watch ye and pray, lest ye enter into temptation' (Mark 14:38). Watch against the stealthy approach of the enemy, watch against old habits and natural inclinations, lest they assert themselves; force them back, and watch. Watch the thoughts, watch the plans, lest they become self-centered. Watch over the souls whom Christ has purchased with His own blood. Watch for opportunities to do them good.

"Watch, 'lest coming suddenly he find you sleeping' (Mark 13:36)." [13]

There has been a voice among us. And if we will heed it, we may yet be led out of the world of waiting and into the Promised Land.

Notes

[1] *The Desire of Ages*, p. 571.
[2] *Ibid.*, p. 578.
[3] *Testimonies*, vol. 1, pp. 179-181.
[4] *Ibid.*, p. 181.

[5] *Ibid.*
[6] *Ibid.,* pp. 181, 182.
[7] *Ibid.*
[8] *Ibid.,* pp. 182, 183.
[9] *Ibid.,* p. 183.
[10] *Ibid.,* p. 184.
[11] *Testimonies,* vol. 5, p. 77.
[12] *Ibid.,* vol. 6, pp. 404, 405.
[13] *Ibid.,* pp. 405-410.